Marianne—

PLEASE READ THIS
BOOK TO MY GOOD
FRIEND Jack.

THIS BIOGRAPHY IS ABOUT
A MAN WHO DID THE
ORDINARY THINGS IN LIFE,
EXTRAORDINARILY WELL.

Doug

saxum

THE LIFE OF
ALVARO DEL PORTILLO

saxum
THE LIFE OF
ALVARO DEL PORTILLO

JOHN F. COVERDALE

Scepter

Published by Scepter Publishers
P.O. Box 1391
New Rochelle, NY 10802
www.scepterpublishers.org

Text and cover design by Rose Design

Printed in the United States of America

Library of Congress Cataloging-in-Publication Data

Coverdale, John F., 1940–
    Saxum : the life of Alvaro del Portillo / John F. Coverdale.
        pages cm
    ISBN 978-1-59417-214-4 (hardback : alk. paper)
    1. Portillo, Alvaro del. 2. Catholic Church-Spain—Clergy—Biography.
3. Opus Dei (Society)—History. l. Title.
8X4705.P65763C68 2014
267'.182092—dc23
tBI
                                                    2014017566

To the memory of Lynn Coverdale

CONTENTS

NOTE ON SOURCES

The most important published source for information on the life of Don Alvaro is Javier Medina Bayo's eight-hundred-page biography, *Alvaro del Portillo. Un hombre fiel* (Madrid: Ediciones Rialp, 2013). I also found useful Salvador Bernal's *Recuerdo de Alvaro del Portillo, Prelado del Opus Dei* (Madrid: Ediciones Rialp, 1996), published in English under the title *Alvaro del Portillo* (New York: Scepter Publishers, 1999), and Hugo de Azevedo's, *Missão cumprida: biografia de Alvaro del Portillo* (Lisbon: Diel, Ltd., 2008).

I am grateful to the prelate of Opus Dei, Bishop Javier Echeverría, for taking the time to answer my questions, and to Fr. Francesc Castells for orienting me during my research in the archives of the Prelature of Opus Dei, where I focused on Don Alvaro's correspondence and on testimonies from people who knew him.

María Eugenia Ossandón was kind enough to permit me to use her article "Los encuentros entre mons. Alvaro del Portillo y Juan Pablo II" (forthcoming in the review *Studia et Documenta*), which provided helpful information on the relations between del Portillo and St. John Paul II.

Readers who would like information about any particular fact mentioned in this book can direct inquiries to the author via e-mail to *coverdale.john@gmail.com*.

INTRODUCTION

L ate in the afternoon of March 23, 1994, St. John Paul II
arrived at Opus Dei's headquarters in Rome for the wake
of Bishop Alvaro del Portillo, the prelate of Opus Dei, who
had died early that morning.[1]

In the Prelatic Church of our Lady of Peace, where the
wake was being held, John Paul II knelt and prayed for ten
minutes. When the Pope rose, the vicar general of Opus Dei
invited him to say the customary prayers for the dead, but
he preferred to pray the Hail Holy Queen followed by three
Glory be to the Fathers and the invocation "Eternal rest
grant unto him, O Lord." When the vicar general thanked
him in the name of Opus Dei for coming to the wake, the
Holy Father responded in Italian, "*Si doveva. Si doveva.*" "I
had to come. I had to."

Why did the Pope feel he had to come to the wake of
Bishop del Portillo?

The principal motive may have been friendship. Del
Portillo had demonstrated a lifelong capacity for friendship, and for many years St. John Paul II had counted him
among his close personal friends. Another motive may have
been a sense of gratitude for del Portillo's many services to
the Church over the course of his long life. St. Josemaría
Escrivá, the founder of Opus Dei, had often said Opus Dei's
only ambition was "to serve the Church as the Church
wants to be served," and Bishop del Portillo learned that

---

1. Opus Dei means "Work of God." Opus Dei is often referred to simply as "the Work."

lesson well. He was a man of great talent and personal gifts, all of them used fully in the service of the Church.

Finally, John Paul may have wished to pay tribute to a holy man. Throughout his life, del Portillo gave a quiet but impressive witness to the great Christian virtues of faith, hope, and charity, as well as the natural virtues that make a man or woman an outstanding human being. He exhibited fortitude, patience, humility, concern for others, and affection. Above all, his life reflected the virtue of fidelity: fidelity to God, to his personal vocation to Opus Dei, and to its founder, whom he supported unwaveringly from the time they met in 1935 until Escrivá's death in 1975. During the next twenty years, he continued to demonstrate as the head of Opus Dei complete fidelity to the founder's spirit, which he saw as God's will for him.

The life of Alvaro del Portillo is an extended lesson in turning the events of daily life into occasions of drawing close to God and bringing others closer to him. Its message is that sanctity and the Christian virtues, far from being somber, are sources of joy and happiness. It demonstrates the effectiveness in the service of God of cheerful self-giving and forgetfulness of self.

Escrivá had a phrase from the book of Proverbs sculpted above the door of Don Alvaro's[2] office: "*Vir fidelis multum laudabitur*"—"The faithful man shall be highly praised." His life is capable of moving others to greater fidelity to their own personal vocations. However different the circumstances of our lives may be from his, del Portillo's example of fidelity and so many other virtues can speak to us all.

---

2. In Spain it is common to refer to priests, older men, and others who merit special respect by their first name preceded by the honorific "Don." From quite early on, the members of Opus Dei began to speak about del Portillo as "Don Alvaro." In referring to him after his ordination, I will sometimes call him Don Alvaro.

CHAPTER 1

FINDING THE MEANING OF HIS LIFE

One day in March 1935, Alvaro del Portillo got to talking with some other students involved in the St. Vincent de Paul Society about a young priest who was becoming known in Madrid for his work with college students, Father Josemaría Escrivá. Manuel Pérez, who had introduced del Portillo to the St. Vincent de Paul Society, offered to introduce him to Escrivá as well. A few days later he took him to the DYA residence in Ferraz Street, at that time the only center of Opus Dei.[1] Alvaro was struck by the young priest's cheerfulness and by the fact that Escrivá remembered things del Portillo's aunt had told him about him four years earlier. Escrivá even recalled her saying that Alvaro liked bananas very much, but that as a small child he had trouble pronouncing the word. Above all, del Portillo was impressed that, although he was still a student, Escrivá seemed to take him seriously. This first meeting lasted only a

---

1. Centers of Opus Dei take many shapes and sizes. Typically they include a residence for some members of the Work and an oratory and usually have a resident chaplain. They carry out a wide variety of apostolic activities. DYA was a university residence housed in several apartments in a building on Ferraz Street in Madrid. It provided lodging and meals in a homelike environment to members of Opus Dei and other students at the University of Madrid. It offered classes on Christian life as well as days of recollection, retreats, and meditations held in its oratory. In addition it sponsored specialized classes in law, architecture, and other subjects.

few minutes. They made an appointment to get together five days later, but Escrivá did not keep it. "He stood me up," del Portillo later said. He assumed Escrivá had received an urgent sick call and could not reach him because he did not have his phone number.

Del Portillo did not attempt to see Escrivá again until three months later, after classes had ended. On Saturday July 6, 1935, the day before he was scheduled to leave Madrid for a summer vacation, he went to the DYA residence to say good-bye, and they "talked at length about many things." As he was about to leave, Escrivá invited him to attend a day of recollection scheduled for the next day. Del Portillo decided to delay his departure and attended the day of recollection.

Opus Dei

We do not know what Escrivá told Alvaro during their conversation on July 6, but it is reasonable to think he explained the spirit of Opus Dei, which he had founded seven years earlier. In the foundational vision he received on October 2, 1928, God conveyed a message about the universal call to sanctity, and gave him a mission to promote within the Church the institution he would eventually call Opus Dei. The message and the institution were two aspects of a single reality. The institution's goal would be to spread the message and help people to live it. It would be made up of people who had received a vocation to incorporate the message into their lives and spread it by word and example.

The heart of the message was the understanding that Christ calls all his followers, not just a select few, to strive for holiness. Escrivá saw, not as a mere theoretical possibility but as a practical reality, that all men and women can and should aspire to love God with their whole hearts, minds, and souls and to love their neighbor as themselves.

In other words, he grasped that God calls all the baptized to the fullness of charity.

At the same time, Escrivá understood clearly that for the vast majority of Catholics, the vocation to sanctity is not linked to a call to become a priest, monk, or nun but to sanctify themselves in the normal settings of daily life. He saw that Christ has redeemed and sanctified all of creation and calls most men and women to live out the great commandments of love of God and love of neighbor in their work, family life, recreation, and other activities. People from all walks of life are called to sanctity—not despite having to live in the world but precisely in and through the situations and activities that come with living there. As Escrivá would write in his book *The Way*, "Your duty is to sanctify yourself. Yes, even you. Who thinks that this task is only for priests and religious? To everyone, without exception, our Lord said: 'Be perfect, as my heavenly Father is perfect.'"

The foundational vision also made it clear to Escrivá that sanctity is not an individualistic pursuit. It is intimately bound up with apostolate—that is, with the effort to bring others closer to Christ; and every Catholic is called to help others get to know Christ, love him, and incorporate his doctrine into their lives. Furthermore, this effort to help friends, relatives, and colleagues live deeper, more authentic Christian lives is not something set apart from daily work and the rest of everyday life. Work, family life, and recreation are instead the settings in which apostolate is to be done and often provide the means for it. In Escrivá's words, "For a Christian, apostolate is . . . not something added onto his daily activities and his professional work from the outside. . . . We have to sanctify our ordinary work; we have to sanctify others through the exercise of the particular profession that is proper to each of us, in our own particular state in life."

At the time of Opus Dei's founding, many Catholics were seeking ways of making society more Christian. They were working to develop Catholic Action and other groups engaged in promoting social and civic action inspired by Christian principles. The message Escrivá received, however, focused not on changing social structures but on encouraging Catholics to make a serious effort to achieve sanctity in their daily activities. In his view, the transformation of social structures and the development of a more just society are expected, welcomed, and desired consequences, but the central point is the sanctification of individuals. He wrote in *The Way*, "A secret, an open secret: These world crises are crises of saints. God wants a handful of men 'of his own' in every human activity. And then . . . *'pax Christi in regno Christi*—the peace of Christ in the kingdom of Christ.'"

The foundational vision Escrivá had received required a group of people within the Church, starting with Escrivá himself, who would dedicate themselves to incorporating the message into their own lives and helping others do the same. As a part of the Church at the service of that message—a part that would come to be called Opus Dei—their role would be both to spread the message and to help people put it into practice.

As Escrivá saw it on that day in 1928, Opus Dei was not to be a mere association to which people would dedicate part of their time and energies for a limited period; rather, belonging to Opus Dei would involve a complete personal commitment in response to a specific divine vocation. In his words: "To dedicate oneself to God in Opus Dei does not mean choosing to do certain things, nor does it mean devoting some of our time to doing good works, instead of doing other things. Opus Dei affects our whole life." A vocation to Opus Dei involves "doing Opus Dei by being Opus Dei oneself," so as to be able to tell "all souls with the example of [one's] life and word that there is a universal call to Christian perfection, and that it is possible to obtain it."

The foundational grace was intended for people of all walks of life, both married and single, and Escrivá's earliest efforts to develop Opus Dei were directed to a wide range of people. Soon, however, he concluded that to take root in all sectors of society, Opus Dei needed first to develop a core of people free to dedicate substantial amounts of time to its apostolic activities and with the educational background needed to give theological and spiritual formation to others. Therefore, he began to focus his attention on college students and recent graduates to whom he presented the ideal of a life of apostolic celibacy in the midst of the world. This was his vocational challenge to del Portillo.

It probably did not include any reference to the possibility of eventually becoming a priest. In Opus Dei today, a small percentage of the celibate lay members are asked by its prelate—usually quite a few years after joining—whether they would like to be ordained priests and continue living their vocation to sanctify daily work as priests of Opus Dei. In 1935, however, no one had ever been ordained as a priest of Opus Dei. Escrivá himself had been ordained in the diocese of Zaragoza. It is not clear whether he had yet communicated to any of the members of the Work his conviction that eventually it would have to ordain priests of its own drawn from among its lay members; thus it seems highly unlikely that when he joined Opus Dei, Alvaro had any thought of eventually becoming a priest.

As Old as the Gospel, and Like It, New

The ideal of seeking sanctity and doing apostolate in daily work which Escrivá presented to Alvaro on July 6, 1935, was, as the founder often said, "as old as the Gospel." Christ himself had challenged all his followers to "be perfect as your heavenly Father is perfect" (Mt 5:48), and St. Paul had told the first Christians at Thessalonica: "This is the will of God, your sanctification" (1 Thes 4:3). At least since St. Francis de Sales' *Introduction to the Devout Life* in the early seventeenth century, Catholic theology had recognized that, in theory, lay men and women could lead intense spiritual lives that brought them to the fullness of the love of God and neighbor that is sanctity.

Yet the message was, in Escrivá's words, also "like the Gospel always new." Although few would have denied that it was theoretically possible for laypeople to achieve sanctity, fewer still proposed sanctity in the world as an achievable ideal. A more intense spiritual life in a young man or woman, or even a desire to serve God seriously, was normally taken as an unequivocal sign of a vocation to the priesthood or the religious life. Few priests encouraged laypeople to make a serious effort to achieve sanctity in their ordinary lives. This reflected a practical conviction that the best to be hoped for from lay men and women was the fulfillment of their basic spiritual duties and the obligations of their state in life. Sanctity in the middle of the world might be an interesting topic for theological speculation, but it was rarely preached about and even less frequently actively pursued. In fact, most people who heard about it from Escrivá in the mid-1930s thought the notion was crazy, if not heretical.

Responding to God's Call

But Alvaro was completely taken with this vision of a life placed entirely at God's service, seeking to come close to him and to bring others closer to him in the setting of ordinary life, which in his case meant life as a civil engineer. During the day of recollection on Sunday, July 7, 1935, a member of the Work proposed that he join Opus Dei. Although Alvaro had had very little contact with Opus Dei, he was, his leading biographer writes, "prepared to hear God's call. The Christian formation that he had received at home and in school, his simple but intense life of piety, his desire to work and to serve those in need, combined with the prayer and sacrifice of Escrivá, had prepared his soul and made it fertile ground for receiving the divine seed."

All that is true, yet this rapid decision to commit his entire life to God in apostolic celibacy, in a fledgling organization with no standing in the Church, was quite uncharacteristic. From boyhood, he had been known for pondering decisions carefully. Clearly he had received an extraordinary grace closely linked to the early beginnings of Opus Dei. He himself observed: "It was evidently a divine call because a vocation of this sort had never even occurred to me. I was thinking only about earning my doctorate in engineering and starting a family." He called the grace he received that day a "knock down grace that moved me to respond, 'Lord, here I am. I want to belong to the Work.'"

To formalize his decision, he wrote a very brief letter to Escrivá dated July 7, 1935. Addressing him as "My dear Father," he limited himself to this: "Having come to know the Work of God, I write to you to ask you to allow me to join it. I entrust myself to your prayers to persevere in this resolution."

Who was this engineering student who joined Opus Dei in July 1935, who would soon become its founder's closest collaborator, and would eventually be his first successor?

CHAPTER 2

EARLY LIFE

A lvaro del Portillo was born on March 11, 1914, the third child of Ramón del Portillo and Clementina Diez de Sollano. Over the next thirteen years, his parents would have five more children. When Alvaro was born, Ramón del Portillo was thirty-three years old. He was a native of Madrid, who had studied law at the Central University, and was working as a lawyer for an important Spanish insurance company. He was a slim, well-dressed, and well-groomed gentleman, by temperament serious and serene but not severe. He was orderly and kept careful notes of even small items like daily expenses or the weight and height of his children. His punctuality was proverbial: You could almost set your clock by the time he came home for lunch every day. He punished the children whenever necessary, but that did not keep them from being close to him. In later life, Alvaro recalled, "God Our Lord wanted me to be friends with my father, and that obviously saved me from bad friendships."

Like many Spanish men of his time, Alvaro's father was a fan of bullfights and attended them frequently. When he could not make it to the ring, he followed them on the radio. Alvaro, whom he often took with him, inherited his interest in the bulls. As an adolescent, he and a group of friends organized several mock bullfights in which they practiced using the cape against yearling bulls, big enough to be exciting but not yet strong enough to be very dangerous. Throughout his life, Alvaro made conversational use of terms derived from bullfighting.

When Alvaro was born, his mother was twenty-eight years old. She had grown up on her family's plantation outside Mexico City, where she excelled at horseback riding. She studied at the School of the Society of the Sacred Heart in London, where she learned French as well as English. She met Ramón del Portillo during a summer vacation in Spain.

According to her daughter, she was "very serene and calm, characterized by great goodness. But when necessary she knew how to act with decision and extraordinary energy." She attended daily Mass and kept a copy of *The Imitation of Christ* on her bedside table. She rose early in the morning and took a cold bath out of a spirit of sacrifice.

From his parents, Alvaro learned to pray. Besides morning and evening prayers and grace at meals, the del Portillos often said a family Rosary. On Sundays they went to Mass together and then went for a walk in Retiro Park, where Ramón often bought them potato chips and soda. On his seventy-fifth birthday, del Portillo summarized the religious heritage received from his family: "My parents taught me to be pious. My mother instilled in me special devotion to the Sacred Heart and to the Holy Spirit. She transmitted to me special veneration for Our Lady under the title of Our Lady of Mount Carmel and . . . so many other good things!" Even late in life, del Portillo continued to pray simple prayers he had learned as a child. One went: "Sweet Mother, never go away./ Keep watch over me both night and day./ Accompany me wherever I go,/ And never, ever leave me alone./ Since you protect me so carefully/ As my true mother,/ Win for me the blessing of God/ Father, Son, and Holy Spirit."

❋ ❋ ❋

As a result of the Mexican Revolution of 1910, Alvaro's mother's family lost their extensive landholdings in Mexico and moved to Spain. But the financial setbacks had no immediate effect on the del Portillo family. Thanks to Ramón's work as a lawyer and the income he received from inherited property, the family lived comfortably in an apartment near Retiro Park in one of the best residential areas of Madrid. Their apartment was not, however, large for a family with eight children, and Alvaro shared a bedroom with two of his younger brothers.

As a small boy, he was generally healthy, despite suffering an attack of rheumatism at age three. He was somewhat pudgy and markedly mischievous. When a family friend with a prominent Kaiser mustache came to visit, Alvaro whispered to his father that he would like to rub some chili pepper on the visitor's lips. Then, ignoring the paternal veto, he ran up and did just that. His father could not help showing his amusement, but the guest was so insulted he challenged him to a duel. On other occasions, Alvaro got into trouble at home for chasing his brothers and sisters around the house with a stick and hitting them on the legs.

High spirits sometimes got him into trouble at school too. One teacher characterized him on his report card as a "clown," while another described him as "somewhat brusque." Yet another became so annoyed that he seized the boy by the feet, carried him to a window, and threatened to throw him out if he ever did the same thing again.

Early Education

In 1920, at age six, Alvaro started school at the Colegio del Pilar, run by the Marianists, a religious order founded in France in the early nineteenth century. In the Spanish system of the time, seven years of primary education were followed by three years of high school, although relatively few students ever progressed beyond the first seven years and only a small minority completed the three years of high school. The Pilar school offered the full ten years. French played an unusually important role in the school's life, and the children were required to speak it during recess. Alvaro would study at El Pilar for eight years. In the early years he was an outstanding student; later he earned good but not exceptional grades—a mix of As and Bs.

Even as a small child, del Portillo was energetic and determined but easy to get along with. He often went out of his way to help others and showed unusual kindness and understanding. When he was in second grade, a fellow student's spontaneous outburst so annoyed the teacher that he punished the entire class by canceling a planned trip to Retiro Park. Naturally the boy was worried about how his classmates would react, but Alvaro, he recalls, "forgave me with the smile and the warmth that characterized him."

By the standards of Spain in the early twentieth century, the Pilar School laid quite a bit of stress on physical education and sports that included soccer, gymnastics, fencing, hockey, mountain climbing, and tennis. Alvaro took part in sports, but sometimes at recess he preferred to talk with friends. He seems not to have been particularly athletic, although one classmate recalls him as "an excellent defensive player on his soccer team—one greatly feared by the opposing forwards." During summer vacations he enjoyed swimming, horseback riding, bicycling, and sailing.

Between ages ten and twelve, Alvaro suffered various bouts of rheumatism. Although the doctor imposed a strict diet and required him to take unpleasant medicine, he bore the illness cheerfully and with good humor. One day, when his brothers and sisters were having a Mexican breakfast that he was not allowed, he commented with a smile: "You're really lucky. You can have fried eggs and beans while all they give me is medicine."

The religious training at home was reinforced at the Pilar School. Mass was celebrated every day before classes began at 9:00 a.m. Although attendance was not obligatory, Alvaro attended Mass and received Communion regularly after he made his First Communion on May 12, 1921. Church law at the time prohibited eating or drinking anything from midnight until the actual reception of communion, so Alvaro could not enjoy the family breakfast; a piece of bread wrapped in paper and carried in his pocket was his breakfast after Mass. It is not clear whether the school schedule included some sort of mid-morning snack or if that piece of bread had to tide him over until dinner at 2:30 in the afternoon.

His sister comments: "It is difficult for a young boy to begin the day without breakfast. Nonetheless he did it every day as if it were the most normal thing in the world. He left the house without having eaten, with a smile and with just a piece of bread wrapped up in paper in his pocket. 'Alvaro, aren't you going to eat?' we asked him. 'No, no, this is enough,' he responded, pointing to his piece of bread. And he did that one day after another, even when he was still just a small boy."

Alvaro also participated actively in the devotional services at school, including the Stations of the Cross. In later life, he recalled some of the hymns. "For the last station we sang some very bad verses that touched my heart and still do. 'The Lord of all things/Lies beneath the great stone/ but with joy the world rings/for salvation has shown.' How true that is. God dies, so that we might live. He is buried, so that we might go everywhere. Therefore the earth sings the joy of salvation."

Choice of Career

Spanish students had to make career choices earlier in life than their American counterparts. The first year of the three-year high school program was the same for everyone, but at the end of that year, at age fourteen, students had to choose between letters and science. Because both primary education and high school were one year shorter than in the United States, they graduated from high school and enrolled in the university at sixteen. At that point they had to decide immediately on a major, which might be something like medicine or law that Americans would begin only after four years of college.

Students who wanted to become engineers often made that choice even earlier, at age thirteen upon completing the equivalent of seventh grade. That was because engineering occupied an anomalous position in the Spanish educational world. In the 1920s and 1930s, it was probably the most prestigious profession in Spain and one of the most intellectually demanding careers. Even so, the engineering school, which had begun as a service school for the army, did not technically form part of the university. Completion of high school, required for admission to the university, was therefore not required for admission to the engineering school. In theory, a student who had completed only the seven years of primary school could enter engineering if he could pass the entrance exam. But that exam required a thorough knowledge of science and mathematics at a level well beyond what was taught in high school, to say nothing of primary school.

Students bent on engineering therefore usually did not attend a regular high school. Instead they enrolled in a private academy offering a higher level of instruction in math, science and other subjects, with a focus on areas necessary to pass the entrance exam for the engineering school. Most students spent at least two years studying in one of these academies, and many spent four or five years there. In the end, they did not receive a high school degree, although they were much better versed in math and science than their contemporaries who had studied science in a high school. Yet, even with years of specialized training, the entrance exam to the engineering schools was daunting.

After seventh grade, about a dozen of Alvaro's classmates who were planning on going into engineering or attending a military academy decided not to continue on with the three years of high school but to enroll in one of the private academies. Alvaro, however, remained at El Pilar for the first year of high school, suggesting that he had not yet have decided on engineering as a career. Law was another possibility, since his father was a lawyer. Later he explained that he decided against law because he was shy and did not like speaking in public. He thought he was better suited for a field where he could work alone.

During his first year of high school, he decided to try to gain admission to the School of Civil Engineering. Other than his having rejected law, not much is known about how he reached this decision. A talent for drawing and the fact that El Pilar had a tradition of sending students into engineering may have been factors.

His choice of engineering was daring and in some ways puzzling. It was far from clear that he would pass the notoriously difficult entrance exam. Only about 4 to 5 percent of those who applied each year were admitted, and Alvaro's grades did not suggest the outstanding abilities in math and science required to make getting into the engineering school a realistic hope. In his first year of high school, he got a C in math. He had gotten an A in physics and chemistry in seventh grade, but in sixth grade he had received Bs in arithmetic and geography.

The decision probably was not made lightly. Facing decisions much less important, he often said, "I'll think about it." A relative who knew him at the time says that for him this was no mere excuse for not making a decision on the spot but reflected a real determination to think things through. His decision seems to reflect a high degree of self-confidence as well as a willingness to work very hard.

Preparation for Engineering School

Alvaro entered the Misol academy in fall 1928 at the age of fourteen to begin preparing for the engineering school entrance exam. It was five years later, in 1933, when he finally achieved his goal. Those five years were filled mainly with classes and long hours of study.

On September 23, 1928, his older brother invited him to go to the theater, but at the last minute he changed his plans. During the performance, a fire broke out and seventy-seven people were killed in the rush for the exits. One summer day three or four years later, Alvaro agreed to go out with one of his brothers and some friends on a motorboat. When they were already in the boat and about to put out, his brother felt ill, and Alvaro decided to remain behind with him. The boat sank in a sudden storm, and all but one of their friends drowned. Alvaro believed God had saved his life for some special reason, although he did not think the reason involved the priesthood or the religious life. Becoming an engineer, marrying, and raising a family remained his plan.

He continued to attend daily Mass even during summer vacations and often made a visit to the Blessed Sacrament on his way home in the evening, but with the exception of the St. Vincent de Paul Society, he did not join any of the numerous Catholic groups that proliferated in Spain at the time, or even become an altar boy.

God made himself felt in Alvaro's life not only in dramatic events like his two close calls but also in more quiet ways. During summer vacations in small coastal towns in the north of Spain, he discovered in the beauty of the landscape, particularly the ocean, the beauty of God. Looking out over the water or rowing out from shore, he learned to pray, speaking with God and thanking him for creating such beauty. "And it was at that time," he said later, "that our Lord began to enter my heart."

Despite the heavy demands studies made on his time, Alvaro took an active interest in his younger brothers and sisters, helping them put together puzzles and entertaining them in other ways. On one occasion, he got his younger brother to pose for several photographs and amazed him a few days later with a picture of him shaking hands with himself, no mean feat with an old Kodak camera many decades before digital editing.

He showed great patience in dealing with his siblings. One day his youngest brother, Carlos, knocked over a bottle of ink and spoiled a set of drawings on which Alvaro had labored a long time. When Alvaro returned home, he sat little Carlos on his knee and talked to him about being more responsible. Carlos was astonished and greatly relieved. "Instead of hitting me," he later recalled, "what he did was just explain to me how important that work was, so that from then on I would learn to be more careful!"

Entrance Exams

Alvaro took the entrance exam for the school of civil engineering, as well as for the school of mining engineering, for the first time in spring of 1932 at the age of eighteen. He was not accepted by either school, although he came closer to passing the exam for mining engineering.

Students often took this entrance exam several times, and he did not abandon his goal of becoming a civil engineer. But feeling a need to begin earning money promptly in order to help his family, then facing economic difficulties because of losses his father had suffered in the early years of the Depression, he decided to begin a two-and-a-half year program in public works engineering technology in the School of Public Works Engineering Technology whose graduates were eligible for positions in the Ministry of Public Works. The school was situated in the same building as the School of Civil Engineering and the two schools shared faculty members.

In October 1932, Alvaro passed the entrance exam for this school and began studying engineering technology, while continuing to spend much time preparing to retake the entrance exam in civil engineering. In spring 1933 he finished his first year in engineering technology with a grade of pass on a scale of high pass, pass, and fail. At the same time, he passed the entrance exam for the civil engineering school. He was one of twenty-three candidates admitted out of 549 who took the exam.

In the fall of 1933, Alvaro began first year of civil engineering while continuing to study public works engineering technology. It was possible to do both because the classes in civil engineering were taught in the morning and those in engineering technology in the afternoon. After a short time, however, he was told he had to choose one or the other. He had spent five years preparing to study civil engineering. It was far more prestigious than engineering technology and would eventually pay much better. But he wanted to help his family financially, and it would be five years before he would begin earning money as a civil engineer, whereas in a little more than a year he could get a job as an engineering technician. He opted to postpone his studies of civil engineering.

By the fall of 1934, Alvaro had finished his course work in engineering technology, although he still had to complete a final project. While working on the project, which he finished in January 1935, he began the first year of civil engineering. Several months later, he got a job in a government office, working in the afternoon and continuing his civil engineering studies in the morning.

Bringing Others Closer to God

On the way home from school, Alvaro usually talked with friends who were going in the same direction. Often, but with no visible success, he talked about religion with one who professed to be an agnostic. In the years that followed, the two friends continued to exchange letters, and Alvaro always included a "Pray for me" in his. In one of his friend's last letters to del Portillo, he said, "Not to worry—this family does indeed pray for you." Before his death, the man received the sacraments.

A fellow student at the School of Civil Engineering, Manuel Pérez Sánchez, introduced Alvaro to a group of ten or twelve young men active in the St. Vincent de Paul Society. Most were engineering students. The group included Pedro Arrupe, the future president general of the Jesuits, and Jesús Gesta de Piquer, who would die a martyr three years later at the start of the Spanish Civil War and be beatified by St. John Paul II. Members of this group later recorded their recollections of Alvaro. One described him as "tall, refined, with an understanding and serene gaze and a smiling face." Another recalled that he was pious, with a desire to bring others closer to God and to help the needy. His character, he said, was extremely straightforward, serene, and prudent.

The students went frequently to the poorest neighborhoods to distribute alms, medicine, and food coupons. They also taught religion to children there and organized a retreat for men, which essentially consisted of catechism classes. At the end of the retreat, they acted as waiters at a dinner for the participants.

One day they went to visit a family that lived in a shanty and discovered that the police had arrested both parents, leaving behind four small children who had no food and were shivering from cold. Alvaro and his friends went to the local police station, only to find it closed. They gave money to a neighbor to buy food for the children and promised to come back the next day. When they returned in the morning, they found the police uninterested in the problem. Lacking any better solution, they decided to take the children to an asylum. One child was too small to walk, so Alvaro carried him in his arms.

Many inhabitants of the area were violently anticlerical and resented the well-to-do young men who were attempting to bring a Christian message to their neighborhood. On February 4, 1934, a group of them attacked the students as they were coming out of a catechism class. One hit Alvaro on the head with a wrench. Alvaro escaped into a nearby subway station, where he managed to get into a train just before it left, leaving his assailants behind. When he got home, his coat covered with blood, his parents were out. To avoid frightening his younger brothers and sisters, Alvaro said he had fallen in the street. The first aid station to which he went botched the job, and he developed an infection that required long and painful treatment from the family doctor, who commented to his mother, "What a brave son you have! He never complains."

Despite the obvious danger of returning to the neighborhood, Alvaro continued to go there, both to teach catechism and to bring some relief to a least a few of the slum dwellers. Years later, he said of the people he met there: "I always learned from them. They didn't even have enough to eat, but I always saw them happy. For me it was a great lesson."

To understand this period of Alvaro's life and especially his adventures during the Spanish Civil War, we need to leave him for a moment and turn our attention to the dramatic events then occurring in Spain.

CHAPTER 3

POLITICAL AND SOCIAL BACKGROUND[1]

S pain in the 1930s was a relatively poor country by Western European standards, and social tensions were acute. Madrid was surrounded by shanty towns inhabited by desperate people who had flocked to the capital despite low wages and precarious living conditions. Workers were divided between a socialist union, the UGT, with about a million workers, and an anarchist union, the CNT, with another million.

Social and economic tensions were exacerbated by bitter religious divisions. The majority of Spaniards were baptized Catholics, many of whom took their religion seriously and were happy to see Catholic teaching influence the country's legislation on marriage and education. But many bourgeois political leaders, who took their ideology from the Enlightenment, as well as most socialists and anarchists, wanted to reduce or eliminate the Church's influence on national life.

---

1. Readers who desire more background might consult John F. Coverdale, *Uncommon Faith: The Early Years of Opus Dei, 1928–1943* (New York: Scepter Publishers, 2002). The material in this chapter is taken from that book. A more detailed account can be found in Stanley G. Payne, *The Spanish Civil War* (Cambridge, Mass.: Cambridge University Press, 2012).

The Second Republic

In 1931 Spain, traditionally a monarchy, became a republic. The change was accomplished without violence. But the monarchy had become identified with defense of the Church for many Catholics, and they viewed the coming of the Republic as a serious threat to their religion. For their part, many supporters of the Republic viewed the Church as the principal obstacle to their plans for social, economic, and cultural reform.

A few weeks after the declaration of the Republic, a small incident in Madrid degenerated into three days of violence directed primarily against churches, monasteries, and convents, an outburst of violence known in Spanish history as the "burning of the convents." The Republican government did not provoke the violence, but was very slow in responding to it. Once it finally intervened, the violence ended quickly, but only after approximately one hundred churches and convents had been burned. The government's lack of action during the early days of the rioting convinced many Catholics that the new regime was an implacable enemy of the Church.

Anti-Religious Legislation

The newly established Republic issued a series of decrees and regulations that upset many Catholics. It established full freedom of conscience and cult; made religious instruction voluntary in state schools; dissolved the chaplain corps of the Army and Navy; substituted a promise for the traditional oath of office; deprived the Church of representation in the National Council on Education; and prohibited government officials from attending public religious acts. In a tolerant, religiously pluralistic society, many of these actions would have faced little opposition. Most Spanish Catholics, raised in an environment of close collaboration between Church and State, however, saw them as hostile to the Church.

During the election for the Constituent Assembly that was charged with writing a constitution, political groups favorable to the Church were in disarray. As a result, parties hostile to the Church won a majority of seats and subsequently dominated the writing of the Constitution. Article 3 declared that Spain "has no official religion." Article 26 went further and provided for the dissolution of the Jesuits and the confiscation of their property.

Legislation passed under the new Constitution deprived the Church of ownership of all churches and monasteries, although it would be permitted to continue using the buildings. Religious orders were subject to severe governmental controls, and their members were prohibited from teaching anything other than religion.

Swing to the Right and Back

By fall 1933, Spanish Catholics and other conservatives had recovered from the shock and disorganization that caused them to make such a poor showing in the elections just after the declaration of the Republic. They formed an electoral coalition that enabled them to present a single candidate in most districts and thus to take advantage of the winner-take-all character of the electoral system that had worked against them and in favor of the parties of the Left in 1931. Conservatives also benefited from the fact that women, who had not been enfranchised in 1931, were able to vote in 1933. By contrast, after two years of fierce fighting in the Parliament, the parties of the Left and Center-Left were so badly divided that they could not present a unified front in the elections.

The swing to the Right in government policies that followed was significant although not dramatic. The vanquished

Left, however, viewed these developments with alarm, seeing them as part of the European movement that had brought Hitler to power in 1933 and would soon lead to the assassination of the Austrian Prime Minister Dollfuss.

For a year, Spain was torn by frequent strikes and a number of small-scale revolts. In October, 1934, the Left called for a nationwide general strike that triggered a revolutionary uprising. The movement failed quickly in most of the country, but it developed into a full-scale revolution in the mining area of Asturias in northern Spain.

To put down the revolts in Asturias, the Center-Right government called in the Army of Africa from Spain's small colonies. This was a desperate move. The Army of Africa was trained to put down colonial uprisings with whatever force was necessary. In the fighting that followed, neither the revolutionaries nor the army showed any restraint. More than 1,000 civilians and some 300 soldiers, civil guards, and police lost their lives. Nearly 1,000 buildings were burnt, blown up, or otherwise damaged.

The uprising in Asturias led to the death of thirty-four priests and religious as well as the destruction of fifty-eight churches. During the previous hundred years, outbreaks of anticlerical violence had occasionally involved extensive damage to church property but not wide-scale attacks on priests and religious. This unprecedented level of violence against persons thus marked a new phase in the history of Spanish anticlericalism.

The political and social situation continued to deteriorate during 1935. The country was suffering from the effects of the Great Depression, and the parties of the Left were increasingly determined to bring about radical change. On the Right, extremist parties were growing in size and virulence. The Falange, which looked to Italian Fascism for much of its political vocabulary and style and part of its program, was becoming a significant factor in political life. On the streets, blue-shirted Falangist youth confronted the youth groups of the Left in increasingly violent clashes.

Prelude to Civil War

Early in 1936, the president of the Republic dissolved parliament and called for new general elections. In preparation for the elections, the working-class parties of the Left and the middle-class parties of the Center-Left united to form the Popular Front. The rhetoric of the Left became increasingly inflamed. Although it now seems clear that there was no real probability of a revolution in early 1936, the Spanish Right was convinced that a Communist revolution was imminent, and the parties of the Left did nothing to assuage those fears.

The 1936 elections brought with them a modest shift in the popular vote from the Center and Center-Right toward the Center-Left. The Popular Front won over 40 percent of the popular vote, the parties of the Right about 30 percent, and the Centrist parties about 20 percent. Neither the Communists nor the Falangists received many votes. In the parliament, however, the shift was far more dramatic. Thanks to alliances among the parties of the Popular Front and the winner-take-all electoral system, the Popular Front won about 56 percent of the seats. The parties of the Right won 30 percent of the seats, leaving a badly fragmented Center with only 14 percent of the seats and virtually no influence.

During spring and early summer of 1936, violence was widespread. Peasants, encouraged by the electoral results, occupied the land in the south. In the cities, there were more and more attacks on public and private buildings, especially churches. Between February 3rd and the beginning of the Civil War on July 17, approximately 270 people were killed and almost 1,300 wounded in political incidents and assassinations.

As spring progressed, the political climate grew increasingly tense. Virtually everyone suspected—as it turned out, correctly—that the Army was planning a coup. Labor unions and political parties on the extreme Left and Right were busy organizing and arming private militias that clashed with one another and created a climate of fear and violence in the streets.

Military Uprising

By early June, a group of army officers had all but completed their plans for overthrowing the government. They intended to establish a temporary military government and call a constituent assembly to write a new constitution. Other than restoring order, their political goals were vague.

The assassination by government security forces of a prominent right-wing leader finally touched off a military revolt on July 17, 1936, in Spanish Morocco. It soon spread to the rest of the country. The leaders were primarily younger officers, because most senior generals either opposed the revolt or were undecided. Significant parts of the army and a majority of the air force and navy refused to join the officers who rose against the government. In many areas, the militarized police (the civil guards and assault guards) fought vigorously against the army units that joined the revolt.

After several rapid changes of government, José Giral, an obscure left-wing Republican professor who had served as minister of the navy, became prime minister. His new government was made up entirely of middle-class liberals, but it enjoyed the explicit support of Socialists, Anarchists, and Communists. On July 19, at the urging of his Socialist and Anarchist backers, Giral took the momentous step of "arming the population" by issuing weapons to the members of Socialist and Anarchist militia units. This decision pushed many ambivalent army units into the arms of the Nationalists.

By July 20, the country was divided into two zones. Forces opposed to the revolt and nominally loyal to the Republican government occupied approximately two-thirds of the territory, including most of the Atlantic coast and the entire Mediterranean coast, except for an area near Cádiz. They held Madrid, Barcelona, and all the other principal cities and industrial centers with the exception of Saragossa in the north and Seville and Cordoba in the south. The Nationalists had gained the upper hand in a large part of the northern half of the country with the exception of the Catalan provinces in the northeast and the strip along the Atlantic Coast that comprised the Basque Provinces, Santander, and Oviedo. In the south, they held only small enclaves around Seville and Cordoba and a strategically important area around Cádiz, which would permit them to move troops into the peninsula from Spain's North African possessions, which they also controlled.

The civil war rapidly became an international event. Both sides promptly sought arms and assistance from the countries they thought would be sympathetic to their cause. As the conflict progressed, both sides received significant aid that helped shape the war: the Nationalists from Germany and Italy, the Republicans from the Soviet Union and France.

Revolution

The Nationalist uprising and the government's response brought about the revolution that the military leaders had feared. Concretely, Giral's decision to give out arms to Socialist and Anarchist militia units helped prevent a quick

Nationalist victory, but it led to an almost complete break-down of the government.

Only in Madrid did the government retain any control over events, and even there its orders were ignored more often than not. Militia units and popular tribunals quickly took control of cities, towns, and country villages in the areas where the Nationalist movement initially failed. Republican legality collapsed in the face of a full-scale social revolution. As the most prominent Spanish communist orator of the time, Dolores Ibárruri (known as *La Pasionaria*), put it, "The whole state apparatus was destroyed and state power lay in the streets." Although the Giral government laid claim to being the legal government of Spain and presented its followers as "loyalists," it bore little resemblance to the liberal parliamentary government foreseen in the Republican constitution. Nonetheless, the forces opposed to the Nationalists are usually called "Republicans."

It would take the Central government months to regain control of the streets in Madrid and the other parts of the country where the Nationalist movement had failed. In the early months of the war, revolutionary committees, whose composition varied from province to province, had far greater influence and power than the Central government. Republican Spain became *de facto* a confederation of regions governed, to the extent that they were governed at all, by Socialist and Anarchist trade unions and their militias, working through juntas of various sorts.

The collapse of governmental control in the Republican zone was accompanied by an outbreak of terror that was primarily the work of small groups from the revolutionary parties who organized themselves for this purpose. The government initially made no serious effort to stop the violence, and in Madrid some of the killing was carried out by police units at least nominally under government control.

Much of the terror took the form of attacks on the Catholic Church and its ministers. Between July 18 and July 31, 1936, fifty priests were assassinated in Madrid and a third of the capital's 150 churches were sacked or burned. Anti-Catholic violence continued unabated through August in much of the Republican zone. During that month, more than 2,000 priests and religious were killed. The violence against priests, religious, and others known to be devout Catholics gradually tapered off after August, although sporadic assassinations of priests and religious continued until the end of the war. By the time the conflict finally ended in 1939, twelve bishops, over 4,000 diocesan priests, and more than 2,500 religious had been killed. One of every seven diocesan priests and one of every five male members of religious orders died. In Escrivá's home diocese of Barbastro, 123 of 140 priests were murdered. It is impossible to say exactly how many lay men and women were killed just because they were known as Catholics, but the number was large. Many of the victims were executed after summary trials before "people's courts" set up by Anarchists, Socialists, Communists, and members of other left-wing parties. Others were simply lynched.

This is the background against which the early years of del Portillo's life in Opus Dei played out.

CHAPTER 4

FIRST STEPS IN OPUS DEI

From the very beginning of his vocation to Opus Dei, del Portillo seems to have received a special grace in the form of a particularly intense sense of being a son of the founder. He understood with great clarity that he could live his vocation to Opus Dei only if he was fully united in mind and heart with Escrivá. In him he saw a model of how to live the spirit of Opus Dei: "Having your feet on the ground and your head in heaven, that is, using all of your abilities to fulfill your daily duties . . . but with your thoughts always fixed on the Lord."

The very day he joined Opus Dei, Alvaro canceled his vacation plans to remain in Madrid for the summer in order to learn to live his new vocation and be close to Escrivá and the other members of the Work. Although the founder was exhausted after a year of grueling work, he immediately began to give del Portillo an entire series of classes, explaining to him the spirit of the Work.

In those classes, Escrivá stressed that Opus Dei was not a merely human undertaking but a supernatural enterprise desired by God. God's intention was not that it should resolve the specific problems of the Church in Spain in the 1930s, but that it would bring the message of the universal call to sanctity to men of all times and all places. Although Opus Dei at the moment was only a small handful of young men gathered around a priest in Madrid, Escrivá talked about it as extending across the centuries and the continents.

From the very beginning of his vocation, Alvaro worked to share with others the gift he had just received. One of these was a former classmate at the Pilar School, José María Hernández Garnica. He had been attending activities at the DYA residence for some time, and members of Opus Dei had talked with him about his possible vocation to the Work, but unsuccessfully. Now Alvaro joined the chorus. Hernández Garnica complained: "Now even that pain in the neck del Portillo, who never used to say anything, keeps insisting that I make up my mind to join the Work." Before July was out, he did join and began attending formational classes along with Alvaro.

Toward the end of August, Alvaro joined his family in the town of La Granja north of Madrid for the final weeks of their summer vacation. Immediately he spoke about Opus Dei to a close friend who was also vacationing there. Because God had called him to celibacy, he stopped going out with girls; his dealings with them remained pleasant and refined, but he avoided long conversations and manifestations of affection.

During his stay in La Granja, he noticed that he had lost some of his initial enthusiasm, and he told Escrivá about it in a letter. A few years later, Escrivá wrote a point of *The Way* that reflected his experience. "'My enthusiasm is gone,' you write. You have to work not out of enthusiasm but out of Love: conscious of duty, which means self-denial."

Plan of Life

At the end of September, Alvaro returned to Madrid to continue working at the Ministry of Public Works and to begin his second year of civil engineering. He worked hard to put into practice what he learned from Escrivá about converting his work and all his other activities into prayer and service to God. Thanks to the formation he received, as well as his personal efforts and the abundant graces God gave him, he gradually acquired a life of intense prayer and union with God according to what Escrivá called "the plan of life" of a member of Opus Dei. The plan consisted of a flexible set of practices of piety that Alvaro would continue to fulfill to the very last day of his life. As the months and years went by, step by step he made them a part of his daily life and struggled to fulfill them with a growing love of God, without becoming discouraged when he found that he had forgotten some of them or had rattled through them with little attention.

At the heart of the plan of life was daily Mass, which quickly became, in Escrivá's words, the "center and root" of Alvaro's interior life. He made heroic efforts never to miss Mass or Communion, even when travel or other circumstances required that he rise very early or extend the Eucharistic fast. This often gave him a severe headache, but it did not deter him from fasting in order to receive Communion or, having become a priest, celebrating Mass when others needed it. At Mass, he offered his work and other activities to God, associating them with the sacrifice of Christ. Throughout the day, when offering his work to God or turning to him in thanksgiving, petition, or reparation, he often joined his prayer to the Mass he had heard that day or would hear the next day.

Another pillar of Alvaro's plan of life was mental prayer. He spent half an hour in the morning and half an hour in the afternoon or evening praying before the Blessed Sacrament. From Escrivá he learned to make his prayer a conversation with God about God and about himself. Prayer meant getting to know God and himself. He learned to talk with God and deal with him as simply and intimately as he talked to his parents, brothers and sisters, and friends. And when prayer did not come easily, he persevered, convinced that Escrivá was right in saying, "Prayer is not a question of what you say or feel, but of love. And you love when you try hard to say something to the Lord, even though you might not actually say anything."

Alvaro nourished his prayer and interior life by reading the New Testament every day, trying not only to understand what he read but to put himself into the Gospel scenes as if he were present at them. Frequently he took from his reading of the New Testament a phrase to use as an aspiration—a short formula of prayer—during the day.

In addition to the New Testament, he spent some time daily on other reading that would help sustain his piety and increase his knowledge of God and the things of God. He read encyclicals and other papal documents, the Fathers of the Church, and spiritual classics like the works of St. Teresa of Avila and St. John of the Cross. He also read contemporary works of spirituality like *The Soul of the Apostolate* by Cistercian Dom Jean-Baptiste Chautard and Benedikt Bauer's *In Silence with God*.

Another important component of his plan of life was daily recitation of the Rosary, usually on his way to and from classes or work. This helped him grow in love for the Blessed Virgin Mary. At times he focused on the words of the Hail Mary and other prayers or on the intentions for which he was offering a particular decade. Habitually he contemplated the mysteries—particular events in the lives of Jesus and Mary associated with each decade—trying in this way to enter into the scenes as Escrivá had advised in his first book, *Holy Rosary*: "We will live the life of Jesus, Mary and Joseph. Each day we will render them a new service. We will hear their family conversations. We will see the Messiah grow up. We will admire His thirty years of hidden life . . . We will be present at His Passion and Death . . . We will be awed by the Glory of His Resurrection . . . In a word: we will contemplate, carried away with Love (the only real love is Love), each and every moment of the life of Christ Jesus."

At noon he paused to pray the Angelus and consider for a moment how things had gone during the morning with the particular point of interior struggle on which he was concentrating just then, while planning how to improve in that matter during the rest of the day. Often this involved trying to sanctify his work, sanctify himself in his work, and make his work a means of sanctification for others. This might call for making better use of his time, working more carefully, or having a greater spirit of service and collegiality. At times he focused on remembering to offer his work for one intention or another: friends and colleagues, world peace, the Pope, the bishop of Madrid, Escrivá, the other members of Opus Dei.

Del Portillo learned from Escrivá to see these and the other practices of piety that made up the plan of life not as scattered moments during the day but as vital elements in the effort to turn work, rest, and the entire fabric of life into prayer—prayer, of course, not in the sense of reciting verbal formulas but as a lifting of the mind and heart to God. He sought to be aware throughout the day of God's presence, turning frequently to Our Lord, his Mother, St. Joseph, and the guardian angels. As a reminder to do this, he liked to glance at the pictures and statues of Our Lady found on many buildings and at street corners in Madrid, taking advantage of the occasion to say an aspiration to her. At work, he often placed a small crucifix on his desk to remind him of God's presence. Frequently, too, he invoked the protection of his own guardian angel and the guardian angels of the people he met.

He took very much to heart Christ's admonition that whoever wishes to follow him must take up his cross each day. He lived traditional Catholic practices of penance like the use of the cilice and disciplines, but his spirit of mortification and penance found expression primarily in small mortifications throughout the day. So, for instance, he stopped putting salt on his eggs. For dessert he had fruit rather than sweets. He drank wine only rarely and did not drink other alcoholic beverages. He refrained from eating between meals and at meals tried to take a little less of what he liked and a little more of what he did not like.

He struggled to be punctual and avoid distractions at work. He reined in his imagination and focused attention on what needed doing at the moment. He bore cheerfully heat and cold and the little setbacks each day brought. He kept smiling when he was especially tired, felt ill, or found a conversation boring or annoying. Most of these mortifications were insignificant in themselves, but lived day in and day out, they helped him come to love the cross of Jesus Christ.

By such efforts to become a man of prayer and sacrifice, Alvaro made rapid progress toward the goal of becoming, in Escrivá's words, "a contemplative soul in the midst of the world."

CHAPTER 5

FUGITIVE AND PRISONER

During the first week of July, 1936, Alvaro and the other members of Opus Dei began moving the furniture of the DYA residence to a new location on Ferraz Street. At just the same time, Spanish army officers were finalizing their plans for overthrowing the government. The army made its move on July 17. In Madrid, the attempted coup failed, but the government quickly lost control of the capital city's streets to armed Socialist and Anarchist militia units that began to terrorize the population, sacking and burning churches and convents and arresting or assassinating priests, religious, and anyone known as a fervent Catholic.

On the afternoon of July 19, Alvaro made his way through the tumultuous streets to the new site of the DYA residence. It was situated directly in front of a military barracks where rebel forces were holed up. On his way back home, he was detained by a militia patrol that discovered a small crucifix in his pocket. It could have been his death warrant, but the militiamen allowed him to proceed.

On the Run

During the first weeks of the war, Alvaro continued living with his parents. Somehow he even managed to keep going to Mass every day until July 26. On August 13, militia units entered the building where his family lived to arrest a general whose apartment was in the same building. The officer was out at the moment, and his wife fled to the del Portillo apartment. The militia followed her with guns drawn. When they saw Alvaro chewing something and asked what it was, he replied calmly, "A piece of paper." He was chewing it to protect the information it contained, but he spoke so matter-of-factly that they took no note of what he said. While waiting for the general, they searched the del Portillo apartment and destroyed the religious pictures and statues they found. When the general finally returned, they arrested him along with Ramón del Portillo who had also just come home. The general was shot the same day. Nothing was known about the fate of Alvaro's father for months.

Because she was a Mexican citizen, Alvaro's mother was able to obtain asylum with her small children in the Mexican embassy. Alvaro, being of draft age, was not allowed to join them. Since he was unwilling to fight for a government that condoned violent attacks on the Church, he was vulnerable to arrest as a draft dodger as well as a practicing Catholic. Unable to remain at home, where militia units could come looking for him at any moment, he found temporary refuge in a house belonging to some friends who were not living there at the time. His brother, Pepe, and another member of Opus Dei, Juan Jiménez Vargas, also took refuge there.

One day in mid-September, Alvaro went to his office, where he was able to collect his salary. On the way home, he stopped to have a beer at an outdoor café—a reckless move that could easily have led to his arrest since militia units frequently demanded to see the documents of people they found in public places. Instead, though, that glass of beer turned out to be providential. While he was sitting in the cafe, the father of another member of the Work spotted him and told him that Escrivá, on the run for two months, had just arrived at his apartment seeking refuge. He was exhausted and on his last legs, but he could not stay there long because the doorman of the building might easily turn him in. Alvaro took him to the house where he was staying.

Alvaro, Pepe, Juan Jiménez Vargas, and Escrivá remained there until the end of September. Escrivá preached to the other three a half-hour meditation every day. Lacking the appropriate bread and wine, he could not say Mass, but he celebrated each day what he called a "dry Mass." Many years later, del Portillo described it. "He followed all the ceremonies of the Mass with a player piano for an altar and his rosary for a crucifix because there were no crucifixes in the house. Religious symbols had disappeared everywhere . . . because being found with a religious image was grounds for being shot. . . . It wasn't a real Mass, because he did not have bread and wine for the consecration. He did it only out of devotion. He omitted the words of consecration out of respect. When the time came for Communion, he said a spiritual communion. The prayers he said were those asking for vocations. . . . He used the Gospel which narrates the calling of the apostles, which he knew by heart."

Since they had no books, they could not spend their time reading, so Escrivá tried to find other ways to keep them busy and help them avoid worrying. Among other things, he taught them a simple card game he had learned as a child which they didn't know. He cheated in obvious ways both to make them laugh and to help them overcome the vanity that can show itself even in a card game where there are no stakes.

At the end of September, they learned that militia units had been searching other houses belonging to the family in whose house they were staying. On October 2, the anniversary of the foundation of Opus Dei, they left for good. For several days del Portillo wandered from house to house, with a toothbrush and a pair of pajamas rolled up around his waist under his shirt as his only luggage. He returned briefly to his family's apartment, and a few days later he obtained asylum in the Embassy of Finland. For his part, Escrivá sought refuge in a private psychiatric clinic run by a doctor whom he had known for many years on October 6.

In Prison

When the Nationalist army reached the outskirts of Madrid, government authorities and militia leaders became concerned the asylum-seekers in various embassies might rise up against the Republic. On December 5 government forces entered two buildings attached to the Finnish embassy and arrested those who had sought refuge there, including Alvaro. He was taken to a makeshift prison established in what had been the San Anton School.

He almost never spoke about his months in prison. The conditions were extremely harsh. The prisoners were badly underfed, and on occasion the guards mixed human excrement in their food.

Prisoners who did not have some kind of pad of their own had to sleep on the bare floor. Meeting one of his engineering professors there and learning that he had nothing to sleep on, Alvaro gave him his pad.

Frequently prisoners were taken out and summarily executed. One day, a militia man stuck a cigarette in the mouth of a saint's statue in what had been the school chapel. When one of the prisoners removed the cigarette, the guard took out his pistol and shot him. On more than one occasion, a guard approached Alvaro, put a pistol to his head, and said, "You must be a priest, because you wear glasses."

Del Portillo was tried on January 28, 1937, and the following day was released. This time the Mexican embassy where his mother and siblings were staying granted him temporary asylum. While in the embassy, he learned that his father was being held in the same jail he had just been released from. His mother immediately began trying to get the Mexican authorities to ask for his release.

Alvaro stayed for about a month in the Mexican embassy and during that time taught classes to his younger brothers and sisters. Eventually, however, the ambassador put him out of the embassy because he was of draft age. After about a week in a boardinghouse, he found refuge in the legation of Honduras.

CHAPTER 6

REFUGEE

The "Legation of Honduras" was a consular office located in the apartment of a diplomat from San Salvador who was serving as honorary consul of the Republic of Honduras. Alvaro was able to find refuge there thanks to the efforts of José María González Barredo, another member of Opus Dei who had been there for some time. The day after Alvaro arrived, they were joined by Escrivá and his brother Santiago. A few days later Eduardo Alastrue, another member of Opus Dei, arrived, and in early April Juan Jiménez Vargas joined the group.

Considering that even full-fledged embassies had been invaded in December, a consular office of a small Central American republic was not an entirely safe refuge. Nonetheless, it was safer than most places. There seemed a good possibility that the Republican government would soon allow people who had taken refuge in diplomatic sites in Madrid to be evacuated. Those hopes would prove vain, and del Portillo would spend the next year and a half in the legation.

The legation was packed with nearly a hundred refugees. The facilities were completely inadequate. Thirty people shared the single bathroom on the floor where Alvaro lived. The meals, consisting mainly of a type of bean used in peacetime to feed animals, were barely sufficient to keep people alive. Often the beans were infested with bugs. Some days there was no food at all.

At first the members of the Work were scattered around the apartment, but in mid-May the consul gave them a tiny room that had probably been a coal bin. It was approximately 8' x 12', about the size of a small bedroom in a modest home. Its narrow window allowed so little light to enter that even during the day the dim bulb hanging from the ceiling had to be kept lit. Thin cushions served as mattresses at night and were rolled up and placed against the walls as chairs during the day.

Most of the refugees did nothing but wait for the war to end, worry about the possibility that the militia might burst in and carry them off, and brood over what they had lost. Thanks to the efforts of Escrivá, however, Alvaro and the other members of the group managed to give "a rhythm of human and supernatural 'normality'" to their time there. Escrivá celebrated Mass every day, using a suitcase for an altar and a crystal glass as a chalice. After Mass, they kept the Blessed Sacrament in a wallet that they took turns carrying. Almost every day, Escrivá preached a half-hour meditation before Mass. His faith, his supernatural optimism, and his good humor helped convert that tiny room into an oasis of peace and even joy.

He urged them to overcome the idea "that negotiating with the talents that we have received from God requires activity and movement. . . . Don't forget that you can be like a volcano covered with snow where the ice on the outside contrasts with the fire that devours it within. It is true that on the outside you are covered with the ice of monotony, of obscurity. You seem exteriorly to be tied down. But on the inside you will be consumed by fire and you will not grow tired of offsetting the lack of external action with a very intense interior activity. . . . From our work which seems so poor will be built a marvelous edifice that will endure down through the centuries."

Del Portillo and the others tried to make good use of their time, mostly studying foreign languages in preparation for the future expansion of Opus Dei. Alvaro studied Japanese as well as German. In circumstances that prevented them from even stepping outside, preparing to go to other countries was a striking manifestation of faith and hope.

Each day Alvaro attended Mass, made an hour of mental prayer, said the Rosary, did some spiritual reading, and observed the other practices of piety that compose the plan of life of a member of the Work. Most people would no doubt have thought conditions in the legation involved more than enough sacrifices, but spurred on by Escrivá's example, Alvaro tried to practice many small voluntary mortifications through the day—adhering strictly to the schedule, greeting irritating situations with a smile, putting off drinking water despite the suffocating summer heat, and many others.

During his long stay in the legation, Alvaro showed great interior balance and supernatural spirit. Forgetting about himself, he poured himself out in acts of service to the others. He volunteered to keep the accounts of the consulate. He bore with sincere cheerfulness the hunger and cold they all suffered, avoiding complaints about all they lacked. In letters to the members of the Work stuck in Valencia since the outbreak of the war, he passed on Escrivá's advice and concerns.

In mid-June 1937, Alvaro and the others learned they had no further hope of being evacuated from the legation. Nor did there seem to be any reason to think the war would end any time soon. Although nationalist troops had gradually occupied some new territory, the balance between the two sides remained essentially unaltered.

The terror of the war's early days had largely dissipated. With documents certifying that he was an employee of the legation, Escrivá could move about the city with relative safety, although still without exercising his ministry publicly. Under these circumstances, Escrivá decided he could no longer remain shut up in the legation. On August 31, he moved to a boardinghouse.

Escrivá thought it would be too dangerous for Alvaro to leave the legation because that would expose him to arrest as a draft dodger. Soon, however, others were able to leave. By the end of October, Alvaro and José María González Barredo were the only members of the Work left in the legation.

By this time, Alvaro's father had been released from jail and had found asylum in the Mexican embassy along with his wife. But he was extremely ill with tuberculosis of the larynx. Dressed as a male nurse, Escrivá visited him regularly and administered the anointing of the sick using holy oils that he carried in a syringe. Although Alvaro naturally wanted to visit his father, he accepted Escrivá's judgment that it would be too dangerous. Isidoro Zorzano was with Don Ramón when he died on October 14. A week later Alvaro's mother left Madrid and moved to the city of Burgos in the Nationalist zone. Soon Escrivá also left Madrid with some members of the Work and eventually managed to escape across the Pyrenees Mountains to Burgos.

When he left Madrid, Escrivá put Isidoro Zorzano in charge of Opus Dei there. During the next nine months, Alvaro repeatedly suggested leaving the legation, enlisting in the Republican Army, and trying to escape across the front to the Nationalist zone. Not until July 1938, however, would Zorzano give his consent.

Alvaro also kept investigating and proposing to Zorzano ways of getting out of the legation and reaching Burgos without crossing the front lines. One plan involved obtaining birth certificates of people of other nationalities in order to get passports that would let them leave the capital. They managed to get Cuban birth certificates and presented them at the Cuban embassy, but the embassy refused to accept them, and the plan fell through.

Alvaro at times felt he was failing to do all he should to join Escrivá and help him with the development of Opus Dei. The urge to try his luck at crossing the lines was very strong, but he obeyed even while finding it difficult. It was hard to fight off a sense of routine and monotony. He clung, however, to the conviction that "although we don't achieve anything, we will not have wasted our time if we do everything we can. . . . Our goal is to help the Father.[1] We can do that by just doing what we can to be able to leave here. So, come what may, we are very happy."

In March 1938, Eduardo Alastrue, who had left the legation at the end of October, returned there after being unable to escape from Madrid. Alvaro found his presence a renewed stimulus to be even more demanding in his life of prayer and in making good use of his time. It helped him, as he wrote in a letter, to overcome the "monotony which the environment was coming so close to introducing into our lives. They should never be monotonous because they are a constant struggle, although it is in small skirmishes. We have reorganized our life, increasing the number of hours we study each day . . . We began to read St. Matthew's Gospel, talking over amongst the three of us what we have read. . . . Even when it seems that all action is impossible, an immense activity is available to anyone who really desires it."

---

1. Members of Opus Dei addressed Escrivá as "Father" and generally referred to him as "the Father." In this book, I sometimes refer to him as "the Father." He established that the head of Opus Dei would always be addressed as "Father" and referred to as "the Father." After Escrivá's death, there was a potential for confusion whether someone speaking about "the Father" meant the founder or the current head of Opus Dei. To avoid that, del Portillo suggested referring to the founder as "our Father" and to the current head of the Work as "the Father." To refer to Escrivá after his death, I generally use "the founder" or simply "Escrivá," but in quotations he is sometimes referred to as "our Father."

As the months went by, the changing fortunes of the Civil War made the prospect of successfully crossing the front somewhat less bleak. One of the people who had been in the consulate had managed to escape to the Nationalist zone. Zorzano was aware of these facts but nonetheless continued to say no. Finally one day while praying, he received a supernatural light from God indicating that Alvaro and several others would successfully cross the front on the feast of Our Lady of the Pilar, October 12, 1938. Escrivá also learned about this in his prayer, and he told Alvaro's mother that her son would pass the front in mid-October.

Crossing the Front

Zorzano gave Alvaro permission to leave the legation and attempt to cross the front, without mentioning what he had learned in his prayer. On July 2, 1938, Alvaro left the legation. His plan was to join the Republican army and cross the lines. A first hurdle was to enlist without being arrested as a draft dodger. The Republican government had called up all men between the ages of eighteen and thirty-one. Alvaro, who was twenty-four, should have enlisted long ago. Even if he succeeded in enlisting without being arrested, he needed to be assigned to a frontline unit to have any hope of crossing the lines.

His only documentation was an identity card issued to his brother, José, by the anarchist labor union. The first time Alvaro presented himself in the recruiting office, he used the name José and claimed to be eighteen. The recruiting officer saw immediately that he was more than eighteen and assigned him to a disciplinary battalion. When they checked his name in the register at the next stage of the process, they found the name of another brother, Angel, listed in the recruiting class Alvaro claimed to belong to. Somewhat disconcerted, the recruiter asked him when his birthday was. Caught off guard, Alvaro gave his own birthday, March 11.

"Well, it says February 14 here," the official replied.

"That's my brother. Notice that it says Angel and not José, which is my name."

"But if you're brothers, how can you have been born in the same year?"

"We're twins."

The official began filling out a new form. "Date of birth?"

"February 14," said Alvaro.

"That's not what you said before."

"Don't be silly. I don't know what I said before, but I know for sure that if we are twins, I was born the same day as my brother."

The officer was so confused he didn't give him any more trouble and assigned him to an ordinary battalion rather than the disciplinary one. The problem was that this battalion was not scheduled for frontline duty, so Alvaro would have no possibility of crossing to the Nationalist zone. He therefore promptly deserted.

Managing to obtain a new ID card in his own name, he passed José's card to Vicente Rodríguez Casado, another member of the Work who had found asylum in the Norwegian embassy. With the new ID card, which he modified to read Alvaro Rostillo, Alvaro presented himself in a different recruiting office, this time claiming to be thirty-one years old. "I asked the guardian angels to take care of things so that I wouldn't be recognized. And in fact, everything went smoothly." Once again, however, he was assigned to a unit which would probably not see frontline duty, so once again he deserted.

Vicente Rodríguez Casado and Eduardo Alastrue also failed in their independent attempts to enlist. In view of their repeated failures, the three of them agreed that "the Lord wants us to put ourselves completely in his hands. . . . Since we don't see any further human means we can employ, the only thing to do is wait for him, who knows more to bring divine means into play and carry us, as if by the hand, where he wants us to go, since we are blind."

On August 18, Alvaro again presented himself to a recruiting office, this time with the name of Juan Alvaro Cortillo. He was assigned to a company scheduled to leave for the front in six days. On the 24th he was able to attend a clandestine Mass in the home of a Cuban family, and from there he left for an unknown destination.

At the end of August, Alvaro was assigned to a new unit where he was reunited with Vicente Rodríguez Casado. A few weeks later, Eduardo Alastrue was assigned to the same unit. In an army made up of hundreds of thousands of men, the three of them, who had signed up at different times and in different recruiting offices, ended up in the same regiment, the same battalion, the same company, and the same squad.

They were aware that crossing the front was extremely risky. More people died in the attempt than succeeded. Among those who had been killed were friends of theirs. Nonetheless, they trusted in divine providence. Whenever there were rumors that their unit was about to be moved, their fellow soldiers speculated endlessly about their destination, but the three members of the Work hardly took part in the conversation. "We are completely unconcerned, because we know that wherever we are taken will be the best place on the whole front for us to cross the lines."

On October 2, 1938, the tenth anniversary of Opus Dei's foundation, Alvaro asked for permission to travel to Madrid for personal motives. He not only received Communion but was able to bring back consecrated hosts so that he and the other two could receive daily communion. On this occasion Isidoro told him that our Lord had given him to understand that they would reach the Nationalist zone on the feast of Our Lady of the Pillar, October 12.

During the following days, they kept the Blessed Sacrament in Alvaro's wallet, which they took turns carrying one day at a time. In the evenings they took a walk during which they made a visit to the Blessed Sacrament. Alvaro, in the account he wrote of their escape, recalled, "We lived intensely the strength and truth of the Gospel narrative about the disciples of Emmaus: 'Did we not feel our heart burning within us, while we walked with him?' To avoid exposing our Lord to the blasphemies and obscenities that were often heard as the men relaxed in the evening, the one who was carrying the Blessed Sacrament that day continued taking a walk until everyone had gone to sleep."

Commenting on a twenty-five-mile march on October 9, Alvaro wrote, "Stops, soldiers who get lost, young boys who swear they can't keep going. . . . But we have the Lord with us, and that leads to expressions of affection, confidence, thanksgiving, exchanges of words of enthusiasm. . . . What a long march for the others, and how short for us!"

On October 10 they reached the front line. The next morning Alvaro, Vicente, and Eduardo were sent to buy some things in a nearby town. With that pretext, they left their unit and began their flight. They spent the night of October 11 in a cave, and the next morning they approached the small town of Cantalojas just as the church bells began to ring for the feast of Our Lady of the Pillar. Two armed shepherds with orders to shoot any unknown person they saw crossing from the enemy lines spotted them but did not fire at them. After being vouched for by Vicente's father, a colonel in the Nationalist army, on October 14 the three reached Burgos, where they greeted Escrivá and Alvaro embraced his mother.

CHAPTER 7

Engineering Officer

While awaiting his first assignment in the Nationalist army, del Portillo remained in Burgos, close to his family and to Escrivá and the few other members of Opus Dei living in the Nationalist capital. He spent the days with Escrivá and the others and slept at his mother's home. In addition to attending meditations, a day of recollection, and talks of ascetical formation given by Escrivá, he had long personal conversations with the founder in which Escrivá revealed aspects of his own spiritual life and even of his mystical experiences. One day Escrivá told him that for many days he had been living in the wound of our Lord's right hand. Entering there he noticed the flow of our Lord's blood and how our Lord was purifying him, changing him, attracting him toward the wound in his side. These insights into Escrivá's personal prayer spurred Alvaro to go deeper in his own life of prayer.

He took advantage of his free time in Burgos to write an account of his crossing the front lines. He helped prepare the informative bulletins that from time to time Escrivá sent to the members of the Work and their friends. He also began writing to people soliciting books for the library of the university residence the Work hoped to open in Madrid once the war was over.

Officer Training School

On November 10, he entered the Reserve Officer Training School located in the little town of Fuentes Blancas, a short distance outside of Burgos. During the Second World War, the American army gave second lieutenants ninety days' training, but under the pressure of the Civil War, second lieutenants in the Nationalist army received a mere sixty days. During those two months, Alvaro both grew in his own spiritual life and brought many of his fellow officer candidates closer to Christ.

The colonel in charge of the school gave him unofficial permission to leave the base for Mass but warned him that if the military police asked him what Alvaro was doing off the base, he would not admit knowing anything. To attend daily Mass in a nearby Carthusian monastery, he had to get up well before dawn and walk several miles along rutted roads in the often biting cold, avoiding the watchdogs of nearby farms. His example was so powerful that soon others joined him, and by the end of the two months, thirty officer candidates were attending daily Mass. Another, whom Alvaro invited to join them, went one day but decided that rising so early and marching in the dead of night to go to Mass was too much. A few months after the end of the war, however, he joined Opus Dei.

Alvaro gave classes to several candidates who were having trouble with the more theoretical parts of the course. He also wrote frequently to other members of the Work and to friends. His letters reflected his ardent desire to begin again the apostolate of Opus Dei in normal conditions. He also reminded those to whom he wrote to pray especially for the founder of the Work: "Remember especially the Father who has so much work to carry out. Those of us, who for whatever reason are close to him, have an obligation to help him in every way we can. The first way, as you know better than I, is to pray and mortify ourselves for him." Whenever possible, he made it into Burgos to see his family and Escrivá.

First Destination: Cigales

On January 1, 1939, Alvaro was commissioned as a provisional second lieutenant in the engineering corps. He was told to report within ten days to a regiment in Valladolid. In the meantime, he filled out the paperwork to be re-admitted to the corps of technical engineers and visited several members of the Work who were in the area.

By this time the war was winding down. The Nationalists had begun an offensive in Catalonia that would soon lead to the occupation of Barcelona. Alvaro was not to see combat. He worked on rebuilding bridges and roads, first near Valladolid in the small town of Cigales, then from April to June in Olot, another small town near the French border in the mountains north of Barcelona.

A few days after arriving in Cigales, he received a letter from Escrivá that read in part, "There are so many great things to do! We cannot afford to obstruct them with childish things that are improper for full-fledged men. I assure you that Jesus expects great services from you and me. I have no doubt we will render them. These days I have been insistently asking our Lord that he give back their enthusiasm for the things of the Work to those members of our family who perhaps do not feel it. Help me to ask for this and to achieve it."

Alvaro set himself a rigorous schedule that permitted him to live completely the plan of life of a member of Opus Dei, fulfill his duties as an officer, spend time with friends, write letters, and even continue his studies of German and Japanese.

Although he spent only a short time in Cigales, he quickly won an excellent reputation not only among his fellow soldiers, who among other things admired his daring in jumping from high rocks into the water, but also among the inhabitants of the town. On one occasion, when a speech had to be given and the mayor was absent, the inhabitants asked Alvaro to deliver the speech. It was such a success that they carried him off the platform on their shoulders.

It was now that Escrivá began to call del Portillo "*Saxum*," or "Rock," in letters. In a letter to him and Vicente Rodríguez Casado dated February 13, the founder wrote, "*Saxum!* I put my trust in the fortitude of my rock." On March 23: "May Jesus take care of you for me, *Saxum*. I know that is what you are. I see that the Lord gives you fortitude and makes operative my word: *saxum!* Thank him for it and be faithful to him." Two months later he reminded del Portillo of the mission that awaited him: "*Saxum!* How white I see the road—the long road—that you still have to travel. White and fruitful, like a ripe field. Blessed fruitfulness of an apostle, more beautiful than all the beautiful things of the earth! *Saxum!*" At the end of June, writing to Alvaro, Vicente, and Eduardo Alastrue, he said: "I know that you are behaving well and that I have in the three of you three rocks. *Saxum!*"

In response to Escrivá's insistence on calling him a rock, del Portillo responded on July 12: "I aspire to your being able to have confidence—despite everything—in the one who, more than rock, is clay with no consistency. But the Lord is so good!"

Escrivá matched his words with deeds and began to rely more on del Portillo. He asked him to write to the other members of the Work and visit them when possible in order to encourage them. He also looked to him for advice: for instance, whether he should ask his mother and sister to take charge of the housekeeping in the residence Opus Dei hoped to reopen in Madrid at the end of the war.

Olot

The war ended officially on April 1, 1939, but Alvaro would not be demobilized for another five months. From April 9 to July 28, he worked in the town of Olot in the Pyrenees mountains about eighty miles north of Barcelona, rebuilding roads and bridges. Vicente and Eduardo were assigned to the same regiment thanks to the influence of Vicente's father, a colonel working in the Nationalist headquarters.

Alvaro was assigned lodgings in the house of a local woman who thought he would make a good match for her daughter. She tried to put him in a compromising situation that would force him to marry the daughter. Far away in Madrid, Escrivá became aware that Alvaro was in a difficult situation and asked the people who were with him at the time to pray the Memorare for a person who needed help just then. Feeling an inner prompting, Alvaro immediately left the woman's house before anything happened. Escrivá later wrote in *Furrow*: "The communion of the saints. That young engineer experienced it vividly when he affirmed: 'Father, on such and such a day, at such and such a time, you were praying for me.'" Since then it has been a custom in Opus Dei to say the Memorare frequently for the member who most needs help.

Alvaro took advantage of every opportunity to spend time with Escrivá. Taking leave the second week of June, he set out for a town near Valencia where the founder was preaching a retreat. The distance was a little less than 300 miles, but railroads and highways had been so destroyed during the war that the journey took him forty-eight hours. Seeing how exhausted del Portillo was, Escrivá suggested he go to bed, but Alvaro insisted that he wanted to attend the meditation Escrivá was about to preach. No sooner had he sat down in the oratory than he fell asleep and began snoring loudly. Many of those attending the retreat were annoyed at the young soldier who, having just appeared on the scene, was now rudely snoring in the chapel. But Escrivá was moved by Alvaro's desire for formation and had no doubt the half-hour he spent dozing in the oratory had gone up to heaven as prayer.

As an officer, del Portillo took special care to see that the married soldiers under his command received leave as often as possible so that they could visit their families. He tried to discourage the blasphemous and obscene talk that the soldiers often indulged in. He also tried to dissuade them from frequenting brothels. On several occasions when his arguments did not convince them, he took advantage of the fact that there were bandits in the area and stationed himself close to the road he knew they would take. As the soldiers approached, he fired several shots in the air. Fearing they were about to be attacked by bandits, they returned to camp.

Although Alvaro commanded his unit only a few months, he won the affection of the soldiers. When news spread that he was being reassigned to Madrid, an unknown soldier painted a rough sign on a wall: "Soldiers, do not weep for the departure of Lieutenant del Portillo. What a good father we have lost!"

He also made friends with a number of fellow officers during those months, including Fernando de la Puente, an industrial engineer who would later become a well-known painter. The two often rode their horses together in the countryside. Seeing a stone wall, Alvaro would say, "I want to see if the horse is capable of jumping it," and go galloping off to tackle the wall. De la Puente, feeling he couldn't do less, would close his eyes and gallop after him, fearing he might kill himself at any moment. Asked why he ended up joining Opus Dei a few months later, he responded that he had grown so used to following Alvaro in those half-crazy feats that he decided to follow him in this vocation as well.

In July 1939, Alvaro was assigned to Madrid and on September 3, he was discharged from the army and returned to civilian life. He was delighted to get back to the capital where he could contribute directly to restarting Opus Dei's apostolates.

CHAPTER 8

SAXUM

In the two years following his discharge from the army, Alvaro demonstrated that Escrivá's confidence in him as a rock on which he could rely was fully justified. He continued to work as an engineering technician for the Ministry of Public Works and completed his studies in civil engineering. In addition, he worked on establishing a new student residence to replace the one reduced to rubble during the civil war, contributed decisively to the expansion of Opus Dei's apostolic activities in Madrid and other parts of Spain, helped form new members, and collaborated closely with Escrivá in the development and governance of Opus Dei.

A Young Engineer

Alvaro worked as an engineering technician for the Ministry of Public Works from September 1939 until July 1941. During most of that time he designed bridges to replace ones destroyed during the Civil War. The ministry had traditionally made provisions for engineering technicians studying to become engineers to attend classes while working. That continued after the Civil War, but combining study with work was now more difficult than ever because the schedule at the engineering school was accelerated in view of the urgent need for engineers.

During the Civil War, all university-level education had come to a halt, and no new engineers had been graduated for three years. In addition, many engineers had been killed or wounded during the war. Now engineers were desperately needed to rebuild the country's infrastructure. To meet the demand as quickly as possible, the engineering school established a special program so students could do two years' study in a single calendar year.

Alvaro began his third year of engineering under this special program in September 1939 and finished it in March 1940. After the briefest of breaks, he attended fourth-year classes between April and October of 1940. Classes of the fifth and final year began in November. Before beginning his last year, Alvaro told Escrivá he was ready to drop out of engineering school, even though he had only one more year to go, so as to dedicate himself more fully to tasks in the Work. Escrivá, however, encouraged him to finish his studies.

Doing three years of engineering classes and finishing a final project in two years while holding a job as an engineering technician was more than enough to keep anyone busy. In addition, Alvaro found time for frequent trips to spread Opus Dei and spent many hours helping Escrivá in the expansion and governance of Opus Dei.

These other activities not only cut deeply into his time for study, but frequently kept him from attending class. Some professors habitually refused to allow students who had missed more than a small number of classes even to take the exam, and one allowed only three unexcused absences. Alvaro had missed many more than three classes. His fellow students were convinced this much-feared professor would make no exceptions. Alvaro succeeded in convincing him to let him take the exam, but exams were oral and his classmates expected the professor would simply fail him no matter how well he answered his questions. But Alvaro passed, and by July he had completed all his exams and the required final project.

Shortly after his graduation on July 15, 1941, del Portillo was hired as an engineer by the Ministry of Public Works. Almost immediately, however, he resigned his position in order to have more time to collaborate with Escrivá. This was in many ways a heroic decision, for he had finally achieved his goal of becoming a civil engineer. The position obtained was prestigious, and a brilliant future lay before him. On the other hand, Opus Dei still appeared to be only a small group of young people gathered around Escrivá. Although enjoying the support of the bishop of Madrid, it had no formal standing in the Church. Its members were only a few dozen people, most of them young, and its activities were very limited. Nonetheless, del Portillo cheerfully sacrificed his career to help Escrivá in building it.

Apostolic Trips

From the very beginning in 1928, Escrivá had envisioned Opus Dei's expansion throughout the world. In 1936, with only a handful of people, he had made detailed plans for beginning in Paris as well as in Valencia, but the outbreak of the Civil War had made that impossible. No sooner had that conflict ended than Hitler invaded Poland, touching off the Second World War. Once again plans for expansion outside Spain had to be delayed.

If Opus Dei could not go to other countries, it could at least begin its apostolic activities in cities other than Madrid. The founder and the other members soon began making weekend trips to Valencia, Valladolid, Saragossa, San Sebastian, and Barcelona, where they met college students, explained the spirit of Opus Dei to them, and helped them learn to put it into practice. At first, Alvaro accompanied

Escrivá on these trips, but the founder soon concluded that his intelligence, maturity, good spirit, and virtues equipped him to take full responsibility for a weekend's activities in one city while he himself went elsewhere or remained in Madrid. From September 1939 to September 1941, Alvaro spent some 200 days on the road spreading Opus Dei's message and giving support and formation to young men who were joining in increasing numbers.

These trips were exhausting affairs. Alvaro and a few others generally left Madrid after work or classes on Saturday and spent the night on the wooden benches of the third-class compartment of a dilapidated train. Alvaro often spent a good part of the night studying in the dim light of a swaying train. On Sunday, he and the others spent the day meeting people and giving talks and classes about the spirit of Opus Dei. They returned to Madrid on the overnight train, arriving in time to begin the day's work on Monday.

A student who attended a talk by Alvaro in Valladolid on one of those trips later recalled his initial impressions: "Del Portillo spoke in detail about the life of piety fostered in Opus Dei. He stressed unity with God through prayer and the sacraments—an intense spiritual life without anything strange, unusual, or ostentatious, a solid piety without externals. For a priest to say this was a novelty. But for an everyday, normal fellow to say it, especially one finishing civil engineering, which then in Spain represented the aristocracy of the University, was cause for endless surprise."

The Church law of that day required fasting from food and water from midnight on in order to receive Communion. Two sleepless nights on a train without so much as a drink of water during the heat of the Spanish summer was a serious mortification. Nonetheless, when Alvaro returned, he was smiling and optimistic about what had been accomplished. Thanks to his generosity and that of the other members, growing numbers of young men joined Opus Dei, and centers soon opened in Valencia, Valladolid, and Barcelona.

Supporting Other Members

Until the end of the Civil War, Escrivá gave personal advice and formation to all the members of Opus Dei as well as to students taking part in its apostolic activities. During the period immediately following the war, the Work's numerical growth and expansion outside Madrid made it necessary that others take over part of this responsibility. Del Portillo was the first to whom Escrivá entrusted the spiritual accompaniment of other members.

In helping them understand the Work and better live its spirit, del Portillo strove above all, as his successor said, "to help them to be very united to St. Josemaría, because he was the instrument the Lord made use of to establish Opus Dei to which they had been called." He was certain Opus Dei was literally God's Work and that his function was to pass on to others the spirit Escrivá had received from God.

An idea of the advice he gave can be gleaned from his letters to members living outside Madrid. He encouraged them to set the bar very high and aspire to real sanctity. In one letter, for instance, he wrote, "Each of us has an unequivocal obligation to reach very high. . . . It is essential that we be as we should be, that we get used to saying no, that we are faithful even in the smallest details." Not content with general exhortations, he went into practical details of how people could live the spirit of Opus Dei in their particular circumstances.

Del Portillo could be clear and demanding. He told one person in a letter that there was no justification for "sadness, feeling lonely, complaining about what doesn't seem to go well, and giving a lot of importance to illnesses." He continued, "Isn't it true that Jesus loves us? Well then? Everything is good because our God is good. Therefore, we should always have joy! It need not be a physical sensation. It is internal peace that should always be reflected exteriorly, for love of God and love of those around us."

He was encouraging, insisting that with God's help everything is possible. One person recalls that when he spoke to del Portillo about a small character defect he found hard to overcome, "he commented that the important thing, in addition to wanting to overcome it, was to be certain that we count on the help of heaven. He told me that when the situation arose I should abandon myself with complete confidence in God's hands. . . . He encouraged me to avoid thinking that it would be impossible to change because . . . it was part of my personality."

Despite his responsibilities in Opus Dei, Alvaro did not give himself airs about his relationship with the founder. So, for instance, he encouraged all members, including those who had only recently joined and were significantly younger, to use the informal "tu" in dealing with him rather than the more formal "usted."

Principal Aide to Escrivá

Escrivá found del Portillo a solid rock on which he could depend. Alvaro had made the founder's spirit fully his own, and put himself entirely at his disposition. In October 1939, Escrivá named him secretary general of Opus Dei. This made him the second-ranking authority in Opus Dei. The appointment was the beginning of his formal collaboration with Escrivá in the governance of Opus Dei, which would continue until the founder's death in 1975.

The new position was a formidable responsibility, especially for a young man of twenty-five. True, Opus Dei was still a miniscule group without any formal legal status in the Church, made up primarily of students and a few recent college graduates in a country with little influence in world affairs. But Alvaro shared Escrivá's vision of it as literally the "Work of God," destined to spread, worldwide and down the centuries, the message of the universal call to holiness in the midst of the world. That it was in its infancy made the responsibility greater in many ways, since a misstep now could have disastrous consequences. But placing his confidence entirely in God, Alvaro was undaunted.

He was in charge in Madrid when the founder was away—which was about a third of the time, since many Spanish bishops asked Escrivá to preach retreats to the priests of their dioceses. Whatever the questions, Alvaro's guiding principle was to do what Escrivá would do if he were present. If uncertain what that was, he responded, "I'll get back to you. I'm going to ask the Father."

Attacks on Opus Dei

As secretary general, Alvaro bore with Escrivá the brunt of a brutal campaign of calumnies against Opus Dei. In the history of the Church, founders of new institutions have often been subject to criticism and opposition even from their fellow Catholics. The founder of the Jesuits was twice imprisoned by the Inquisition. The papal representative in Spain described St. Teresa of Avila, reformer of the Carmelite order, as a "restless, roving, disobedient, and obstinate woman." Opus Dei was no exception.

Even before the outbreak of the Spanish Civil War, Escrivá had been the object of criticism, especially among clerics in Madrid. In response to Opus Dei's growth in the 1940s, the attacks intensified. Criticism came from three distinct groups: some university professors, certain members

of the official political organization, the Falange, and some
priests and members of religious orders.

At the time, professorships in Spanish universities were
awarded on the basis of competitive examinations. Many
liberal and left-leaning professors left Spain during and
immediately after the Civil War, while others were removed
from their posts by the Franco government. This created a
large number of vacancies and made it possible for young
academics to win professorships at a much earlier age than
would normally have been possible. Between 1940 and
1945, eleven members of Opus Dei won university professorships. This was about 6 percent of all new appointments
and of course a much smaller percentage of the total number
of professors. Even so, some who had lost out in the compe-
tition for positions, as well as some established professors
opposed to the presence of committed Catholics on university faculties, accused Opus Dei of attempting to "take over"
Spanish universities.

A much more dangerous source of criticism was found
within the state-sponsored Falangist party. Like the National
Socialist party in Germany and the Fascist party in Italy,
it was the only legal party and dominated political life in
Spain. Some members of Opus Dei, like many other Spaniards, belonged to the Falange, but others refused to join.
Opus Dei encouraged its members to take their civic responsibilities seriously but stressed that they enjoyed full auton-
omy in political matters and refused to urge them to join the
Falange or the student organizations it sponsored.

This respect for political freedom was unacceptable to
some Falangists who demanded the active allegiance of all
Spaniards. They denounced Opus Dei to the Special Tribunal
for the Suppression of Masonry and Communism, accusing
it of being "a Jewish branch of the Masons" or a "Jewish
sect related to the Masons." Today the accusations seem

laughable, but in the highly charged political atmosphere of post-Civil War Spain, this was a very serious matter. The formal proceedings initiated in the tribunal were soon dismissed, but this did not quell Falangist criticism and opposition, which continued for a number of years.

Far and away the most important and painful criticism of Opus Dei came from other Catholics. Many rumors circulated in ecclesiastical circles to the effect that Opus Dei was a heretical organization that would soon be shut down by the Vatican's Holy Office, the successor to the Inquisition. In a convent in Barcelona, copies of Escrivá's book *The Way* were burnt in an *auto-da-fé* ("act of faith") reminiscent of those of the sixteenth century.

Some priests and religious claimed Opus Dei was stealing vocations from the diocesan seminaries and the religious orders. Members of religious orders visited the families of members of Opus Dei, including Alvaro's mother, to warn them that their sons were involved with a heretic and in great danger of losing their souls. Alvaro's mother responded that she knew both Escrivá and her son and was not worried about the accusations. But other parents were deeply shaken. Complaints were also lodged with a number of Spanish bishops and, even more troubling, with the Holy See. In 1941, the General of the Society of Jesus sent the Vatican a set of documents with accusations against Opus Dei.

While Escrivá tried to shield the members of the Work from the controversy swirling around it, he kept del Portillo fully informed, and the young secretary general shared the burden with him. On a number of occasions he was called upon to deal with ecclesiastical authorities who were troubled by accusations that reached them.

One time, for instance, the papal representative in Madrid was told Opus Dei was trying to destroy the Church by stealing vocations from the priesthood and from the

religious orders. He demanded an explanation from Opus
Dei at a moment when Escrivá was out of town. The papal
representative was in no mood to wait for him to return,
so del Portillo met with him. In the face of his accusations,
Alvaro remained calm. "We are all professional men," he
responded. "We earn our living working and have plenty of
money in our pockets. Let me tell you that there are more
enjoyable ways to lose one's soul." The nuncio was disarmed
by the common sense of this response and heard del Portillo
out. Learning more about Opus Dei, he became one of its
most staunch supporters.

Someone once asked Alvaro if relaying messages from
the founder to bishops and even the Pope weighed heavily on
him. Where, the other asked, did he get the courage? Alvaro
replied, "I just keep in mind the miraculous catch of fish and
the words of St. Peter, 'at your word I will let down the net.' I
think about what the Father has told me, and I know that in
obeying him, I am obeying God."

Escrivá also relied on Alvaro for many aspects of Opus
Dei's finances and for setting up its new centers in Madrid
and other cities of Spain. The Work was growing rapidly,
but the vast majority of its members were either students or
recent college graduates, with very limited incomes. Renting
or purchasing new centers and furnishing them stretched
resources to their limits. Somehow they were able to purchase a handsome house in a good neighborhood of Madrid,
but after buying it, money was so short that they could not
get the heating system fixed and spent the winter of 1940–41
without heat. To reduce the cost of furnishing, del Portillo
often accompanied Escrivá to secondhand furniture dealers
and the flea market of Madrid, looking for bargains that
could be fixed up.

Del Portillo often had to do balancing acts to make ends
meet. But instead of thinking they should slow down and

"cut their coat according to their cloth," Alvaro fully supported Escrivá's efforts to push forward quickly despite lacking money. He had taken to heart the founder's admonition to spend on apostolic undertakings "all that you ought, though you owe all that you spend."

A Support in Need

Knowing that Escrivá has been declared a saint by the Church and that del Portillo will soon be declared blessed, one may be tempted to think of both as pillars of iron needing only God's grace and their own strength of character to stand up to the many difficulties they had to face. But it wasn't like that. They were indeed holy men with strong characters, but they also needed human affection and support. Bishop Echevarría, who spent many years with both, says he often observed "how they helped each other mutually, infecting each other with good humor and especially with the conviction that God does not abandon his creatures. From this early period on, del Portillo was, in Bishop Echevarría's words, "the first and great collaborator of St. Josemaría in the work of governing Opus Dei. He became the prudent executor of the tasks the founder entrusted to him and the faithful liaison who relayed to the other faithful of the Work what he transmitted to him to pass on."

Escrivá considered del Portillo's role in Opus Dei providential. "I did not search out Alvaro," he said. "The Lord put him at my side and he, with the help of God's grace, matured humanly and supernaturally. He gave his life with great courage and never pulled back. He maintained a constant positive tone, with amiability and good humor."

CHAPTER 9

A PRIEST OF OPUS DEI

From the start in 1928, Escrivá had understood that Opus Dei was to be made up of both priests and laypeople. He saw clearly that its apostolic activities required the collaboration of clergy and laity. This would not mean lay members contributing to the apostolate of priests, nor priests supporting the apostolate of lay members, but an apostolate carried out jointly by both.

The mission of priests in Opus Dei would be exclusively spiritual: not directing the secular activities of the other members but fostering their apostolic zeal and interior life. As Escrivá wrote in 1931, "The priests will be solely *spiritual directors of souls*, and that is no small thing."

Among Escrivá's earliest followers were several diocesan priests. In 1932, he began a series of weekly formational meetings for them, and in February 1934 a number of them made a commitment to the Work. But these good men found it impossible to grasp fully the spirit of Opus Dei and Escrivá's role as founder. Some were also critical of Escrivá's daring—recklessness, as it seemed to them—in pushing forward the incipient apostolic activities of Opus Dei despite serious financial difficulties.

Not fully grasping the spirit of Opus Dei, a number of those priests sowed confusion among the members of the Work. Things reached such a point shortly before the Civil

War that Escrivá considered terminating their relationship with the Work. In light of their good faith, however, he decided to continue asking them to contribute with their priestly ministry while "keeping them outside the activities specific to the Work."

In this context, he returned to a conclusion he had already recorded in his personal notes in 1930: In the future, the priests of Opus Dei would have to come from the ranks of lay members already formed in its spirit. For the moment, though, there was no possibility of ordaining priests for Opus Dei, and Escrivá confined himself to praying for the priests to come. "I prayed," he wrote years later, "with confidence and enthusiasm during so many years for your brothers who would be ordained and for those who would follow their path. I prayed so much that I can say that all the priests of Opus Dei are sons of my prayer."

In the months immediately after the Civil War, the growth of Opus Dei's apostolic activities made the need for priests more acute. Escrivá spent hours poring over the Code of Canon Law, seeking a way for Opus Dei to be able to ordain priests, but to no avail. The problem lay in two requirements of canon law. In the first place, for a man to be ordained, he must be called to the priesthood by someone with the necessary authority. Under canon law, that could be only the bishop of a diocese or the head of a religious order or some equivalent. Opus Dei was obviously not a diocese, nor could it become a religious order or anything like one. It was concerned with sanctifying the world from within, seeking personal holiness, and doing apostolate in the midst of the ordinary activities of daily life; whereas religious orders and groups like them all involved a degree of what was known at the time as *contemptus mundi*—separation from the world in testimony to its passing character. The second problem was similar.

Once ordained, a priest must be incorporated in a specific diocese or religious order or some equivalent organization.

Del Portillo's Vocation to the Priesthood

Escrivá began thinking of del Portillo as a candidate for the priesthood sometime in 1939. We do not know when he asked Alvaro if he would be willing to become a priest, but certainly no later than spring 1940. Alvaro later recalled how in that conversation Escrivá stressed his freedom to accept or decline the invitation. "If you are well disposed, if you want it, and if you have no objection, I will have you ordained a priest. But you enjoy complete freedom."

There is no indication Alvaro felt any special attraction to the priesthood. From the very beginning of his vocation, however, he had been fully dedicated to "doing Opus Dei, being himself Opus Dei," as the founder often put it. Much as he had been ready to postpone his engineering studies in order to help his family financially, he subordinated his professional goals to carrying out the apostolate of Opus Dei and helping it develop. Given his complete availability and willingness to do whatever was needed, it is not surprising that he said he would be happy to be ordained if the founder wanted that, even though it was not yet clear how or when it could happen. Not much later, Escrivá wrote in his personal notes, "My God, set Alvaro's heart on fire, so that he may be a holy priest!" At approximately the same time, he also proposed the possibility of becoming a priest to José María Hernández Garnica.

While the prospect of Alvaro's and Jose María's ordination was a source of great joy for the members of Opus Dei, many of their colleagues found it shocking, if not incomprehensible. Engineers in Spain enjoyed great social prestige and could look forward to a brilliant future. By contrast, priests generally enjoyed little prestige. Upon learning that Alvaro was going to be ordained, even the bishop of Madrid asked him, "Do you realize that you will lose your identity? Now you are a prestigious engineer. Then you will be one priest among many." Alvaro replied, "Your Excellency, I gave my identity to Jesus many years ago."

In 1941, Alvaro and José María—soon joined by José Luis Múzquiz, a third engineer—began their studies in preparation for ordination. This required enormous confidence in the founder, since they knew he still had not found a way for them to be ordained. The bishop of Madrid agreed that they could study privately and take their examinations in the diocesan seminary without becoming seminarians. They occasionally took off for a week or ten days of morning-to-night study outside Madrid. During one of those periods, del Portillo wrote to Escrivá: "Father, I have great desires to be a good person and to really work within Opus Dei for the Church. What a shame that I so often act like an idiot and fail to do what I should. Pray for me, Father, so that someday I may become a good instrument—a docile one—in your hands."

The Priestly Society of the Holy Cross

On February 14, 1943, while celebrating Mass, Escrivá received what he took to be light from God about how priests could be incorporated into Opus Dei. The solution was the Priestly Society of the Holy Cross—a society of common life without vows, made up of priests and lay members of Opus Dei in proximate preparation for the priesthood. It was far from a perfect arrangement, since a society of common life without vows could easily be confused with a religious order and because Opus Dei might seem to be a part of the newly constituted Priestly Society, whereas in reality the Priestly Society would be only a small part of Opus Dei.

Despite its imperfections, though, this formula represented a workable solution and the only one available at the time.

The bishop of Madrid could not erect the Priestly Society without the previous permission of the Holy See. To prepare the way for the bishop's formal petition, del Portillo flew to Rome on May 25, 1943, to explain to the Holy See what Opus Dei was and what it was requesting. He went armed with letters of introduction from the papal representative in Spain who, after having initial misgivings, had become a firm supporter of the Work.

During the flight, the Italian airliner carrying him found itself in the middle of a battle between British aircraft and Axis ships. Many of the travelers were terrified. Some actors returning to Italy from Spain began to shout, "Mamma mia! This is really dangerous! We are all going to drown!" But Alvaro stayed calm, thinking to himself, "I am going to carry out a mission that God wants, and therefore, nothing will happen."

For the audience with Pope Pius XII on June 4, 1943, he wore the showy dress uniform that Spanish engineers wore on formal occasions because the engineering corps had originally been part of the Spanish army. On his way to the Vatican he was amused to overhear a woman comment, "It's amazing. So young and he's already an admiral!" At the entrance to the Vatican, the officer in charge of the guard also mistook him for a high-ranking military officer. The officer formed the company and invited Alvaro to review it, which he did as if it were the most natural thing in the world, but probably with an inner chuckle.

Little is known about the audience itself beyond the fact that the Pope took a warm interest in what del Portillo told him about Opus Dei and its need for priests ordained from among the lay members. Later, a close papal aide told members of the Work that the Pope was very impressed with the young engineer.

Del Portillo remained in Rome until June 21. His days were so full that in the first three weeks he was unable to visit the major basilicas or the catacombs. He met with many high-ranking Vatican officials, including the secretary of state, who told him that both he and the Holy Father had personally studied Opus Dei's documents in depth because of rumors that it wanted to destroy the Church.[1] Among the officials he met was also Msgr. Montini (the future Pope Paul VI) who became a lifelong friend.

Msgr. Montini was not the only friend del Portillo made during this first stay in Rome. According to one member of Opus Dei living in Rome at the time, despite Alvaro's youth and the fact that he was not even a priest, much less a bishop, veteran officials "listened to him with respect and great interest," perceiving his human and supernatural depth and also "the importance for the future of the Church and the world of the 'novelty' that he was telling them about."

The trip was a complete success. On October 11, 1943, the Holy See granted its permission for the erection of the Priestly Society of the Holy Cross. It occurred on the feast of the Immaculate Conception, December 8.

Preparing for the Priesthood

Escrivá assembled a distinguished faculty to teach theology to the three engineers. In addition to professors from the seminary of Madrid, he called upon a number of professors

---

1. One might wonder why del Portillo would see the secretary of state when the business that brought him to Rome had nothing to do with foreign affairs. The secretary of state, however, is the second-ranking person in the Vatican, charged not only with foreign relations but with overseeing the work of the Curia, the central administrative staff of the Vatican. The secretariat of state has two divisions, one for foreign relations and the other for internal Vatican affairs, referred to as "ordinary affairs." Each is headed by a deputy secretary of state. The secretary of state himself is usually involved to one degree or another in all important questions.

who normally taught in Rome and Jerusalem but had been trapped in Spain by the Second World War. Escrivá himself taught them pastoral theology and trained them in celebrating Mass. Although Alvaro was even busier than during the final years of his engineering studies, he always managed to make time to attend classes and study.

Escrivá wanted Opus Dei priests to hold both ecclesiastical and civil doctorates. He hoped Alvaro and the other two would be able to go to Rome or Fribourg to obtain doctorates in theology, but the war and Opus Dei's urgent need for the services of its few priests prevented Alvaro from obtaining an ecclesiastical doctorate until 1948, when he earned a doctorate in canon law from the University of St. Thomas (also known as the Angelicum) in Rome.

In the 1940s, no Spanish institution offered a doctorate in engineering, so if del Portillo was to have a doctorate in a civil subject, it would have to be something else. For that reason, he enrolled in the school of philosophy and letters. Taking advantage of a rule that permitted "free students" to take examinations without attending class, he obtained a master's degree in history in 1943. Considering the demands on his time, he might have been expected to write a doctoral dissertation based exclusively on published sources, but in fact he did research in the Archive of the Indies in Seville as well as in historical archives in Madrid. In May 1944 he was granted a PhD in history from the Central University in Madrid. His doctoral dissertation, on the first Spanish expeditions to California, won the university's Extraordinary Prize and was published in 1947 with the title *Descubrimientos y exploraciones en las costas de California* (*Discoveries and Explorations on the California Coast*).

Priestly Ordination

Alvaro and the two others were ordained June 25, 1944, in the chapel of the bishop's palace. Escrivá did not attend. He stayed home and celebrated Mass, praying for the new priests. In 1989 del Portillo explained his absence: "Both humanly and supernaturally that was a day of triumph for our founder. . . . He thought that if he went . . . he would be the center of attention. . . . 'My thing is to hide myself and disappear,' he concluded. 'Only Jesus should shine'. . . . His triumph was to offer to our Lord the humility of disappearing, accepting the criticism of some people." At the reception after the ordination, Escrivá tried to kiss Father Alvaro's newly consecrated hands, a custom in Spain at the time. Del Portillo for his part tried to kiss the founder's hands first.

In an informal gathering of Opus Dei members after lunch, Bishop Eijo y Garay told him that when he expressed his fear that members of the Work might harbor resentment against the religious who had criticized Opus Dei so severely, Alvaro had reassured him that they thought of those religious as a platinum scalpel used by the Lord to operate on Opus Dei. Father Alvaro intervened, saying: "But I said that only because I had heard the same commentary from the Father." To which the bishop responded, "Like father, like son."

Late in the afternoon, Escrivá preached a meditation to the people of the Work who had come for the ordination. He said that when years had passed and people asked what the founder said that day, they should reply that he insisted on the key elements in the life of a member of the Work: "Prayer, prayer, prayer; mortification, mortification, mortification; work, work, work."

Confidant of a Saint

For years before his ordination, del Portillo had been
Escrivá's main support and the person in whom he most frequently confided. He witnessed many of the founder's strug-
gles which others were unaware of. On September 25, 1941,
for instance, in the face of bitter, ongoing criticism and even
denunciations to the Holy See, Escrivá confided to Alvaro
in a letter: "I feel very sure that the Work will be greatly
loved by the Holy Father, but after the consecration of the
Mass I felt an inner impulse to do something that cost me
tears. With tears that burned my eyes, as I gazed upon the
Eucharistic Jesus there on the corporal, I told him with all
my heart, 'Lord, if it is what you want, I accept the *injustice*'
I'm sure you can guess what I meant by *the injustice*—the
destruction of the whole *work of God*. I know I pleased him
by saying this and really meaning it. But how could I have
refused to make this act of union with his will, if he was asking me for it?"

Escrivá continued: "Alvaro, pray a lot for your Father
and get others to pray a lot. Jesus permits the enemy to make
me see just how monstrous this campaign of incredible lies
and crazy calumnies is. As a result, the animal man within
me rises up with purely human inclinations. By the grace of
God, I always reject those natural inclinations which seem to
be, and perhaps are, full of a sense of rectitude and justice. I
open the way for a joyful and filial *fiat* [let it be done] full of
divine filiation. I am a son of God! This fills me with peace
and joy, and permits me to forget."

The day after del Portillo's ordination, Escrivá asked him
to hear his confession. From then till Escrivá's death in 1975,
Father Alvaro served as his confessor. Their relationship had
been extremely close, but now it became even more intimate.
The special graces God gave Escrivá demanded a confessor

who himself had a deep interior life, whose spiritual life was in harmony with his, and who had the intelligence and humility to guide him in day-to-day events and in reacting to the graces he received. St. Teresa of Avila's autobiography shows how difficult it can be to find such a confessor. Despite her heroic efforts to find someone who could understand and guide her, she often failed. Escrivá found such a confessor in Father Alvaro, who was constantly at his side and gave him advice not only in confession but whenever he thought it necessary.

To this task he brought immense affection and veneration for Escrivá and the fortitude to make whatever demands he believed necessary. On one occasion, Escrivá commented: "Today Alvaro corrected me, and I had a hard time accepting the correction. So much so that I went to the oratory for a moment and said, 'Lord, Alvaro is right and I'm not.' But immediately, 'No, Lord, this time I'm right . . . Alvaro doesn't overlook anything . . . and that isn't affection but cruelty.' But afterwards, 'Thank you, Lord, for putting at my side my son Alvaro who loves me so much that he doesn't overlook anything.'"

St. Teresa once said every soul, no matter how holy, needs a drain pipe, someone with whom it can give vent to its feelings. Escrivá found it in Alvaro. One night, after they had gone to bed, he called on an internal telephone. "Alvaro, I can't take it any longer." "But Father, we've been saying the same thing for the last three years!" "You're right, my son. Thank you! Good night."

Priestly Ministry

Aside from his ongoing duties as secretary general of Opus Dei, Alvaro dedicated most of his time in the years immediately following ordination to preaching and administering the sacraments, especially the sacrament of penance. A member of the Work who would himself later be ordained a priest recalled that Don Alvaro listened carefully, helped him to see the causes of his sins, and suggested concrete ways of avoiding them in the future. He demonstrated "an understanding that was both kind and demanding." His advice was "wise and practical" and reflected the depth of his own interior life and his concern to do apostolate.

The three newly ordained priests were soon swamped with work. They divided Spain up among them. Múzquiz took primary responsibility for the south, Hernández Garnica for the north, and del Portillo for Madrid and nearby cities. Much of their time was spent giving spiritual direction and preaching meditations, days of recollection, and retreats. Within ten months of ordination, the three priests had given thirty retreats and more than ninety days of recollection.

Father Alvaro was not a particularly eloquent preacher. His style was simple and straightforward, but his deep faith and conviction came through and moved his hearers. He relied heavily on sacred Scripture and on what he had learned from Escrivá, especially the preaching notes and meditation outlines Escrivá had shared with the newly ordained priests.

A biographer who heard him preach frequently observed: "His spoken words went straight to the bottom of people's hearts, largely because the look on his face and the gentle tone of his deep voice conveyed not only the great affection that he felt for his listeners but also an almost tangible humility. In his preaching he was warm, understanding, and affable, but also very demanding. Often he used the word 'more' to communicate the urgency that is inherent in any real love for God. Gently he helped each person to face up to his or her responsibility to love God and souls. This was always his main concern. No matter what he was talking about, everything he said was linked to this one theme: that because the plenitude of Christian life is rooted in charity, love is of the utmost urgency."

A young woman who attended a retreat he preached in 1945 found in his preaching "something new, something distinct. . . . It moved me deeply. Although I had habitually made a retreat in the past, I had never heard anyone speak in the same way about the love of God. It was a great discovery for me, an encounter with God as Father, as friend. It had a great impact on me."

CHAPTER 10

WINNING VATICAN APPROVAL

By 1945, Escrivá began to feel an acute need for immediate Vatican approval of Opus Dei as a shield against the ongoing campaign being waged by certain members of religious orders against the Work. He had hoped that the formal approval of the bishop of Madrid would be sufficient, but that had proved not to be the case. Vatican approval was also urgently needed to facilitate Opus Dei's growth outside Spain. The Holy See had indicated in 1943 that it had no objection to the bishop of Madrid's erection of the Priestly Society of the Holy Cross in his diocese, but as a legal entity Opus Dei existed only as a diocesan society. This had not been a practical problem as long as the Second World War confined Opus Dei to Spain, but with the war's end, it was poised to spread to new countries, and the need for recognition from the Vatican became imperative.

Father Alvaro spent a good part of the summer and fall of 1945 helping Escrivá prepare the documents that would be needed to request papal approval. Escrivá drafted them but asked del Portillo to review them. Alvaro approached this task with a delicate touch, for he was convinced that only the founder had the grace of God to define the norms governing the apostolate of Opus Dei and the spiritual life of its members. He saw his own task as that of an active and responsible collaborator but only a collaborator, whose role was to help the founder.

In early 1946, they began to focus on obtaining letters of recommendation from bishops supporting Opus Dei's request. Since 1939, Alvaro had helped Escrivá maintain relations with Spanish bishops and knew many of them well. During the first two weeks of February, he visited eleven bishops. Although Opus Dei still had no significant presence in many of their dioceses, over half of them agreed to give recommendations.

Father Alvaro Returns to Rome

For at least two years, Escrivá had been suffering from severe diabetes. Now his physician warned that traveling to Italy under the precarious conditions of post-war Europe might prove fatal. Del Portillo fully understood what needed to be done and had repeatedly shown his skill in dealing with Church officials, both in Spain and during his trip to Rome in 1943. Escrivá therefore entrusted the task of trying to obtain Vatican approval to him. On February 25, 1946, Father Alvaro set sail from Barcelona for Genoa. He was accompanied by José Orlandis, a professor of history of law, who had just completed several years' study in Rome, spoke Italian, and knew a number of Vatican officials. Despite the trip's vital significance for the future of Opus Dei, a member of the Work who saw Father Alvaro in Barcelona recalls that he showed no "concerns, much less stress. . . . He demonstrated his usual peace, serenity, and calm based on confidence in God. . . . He was firmly convinced that Opus Dei was from God and was in God's hands. Our Lord was determined to carry it out, and therefore He would accomplish it one way or another."

Letters of Recommendation

The Pope had just created thirty-eight new cardinals, and some were still in Rome. Del Portillo was determined to try to get letters of recommendation from a number of them, including the cardinals of New York, Berlin, Cologne, and Westminster. But they would be leaving very soon, so it was urgent to get to Rome as soon as possible. Another member of the Work, Salvador Canals, who was studying in Italy, convinced a friend of his to accompany him to Genoa to pick up del Portillo and drive him to Rome. By the time the ship docked, it was already late. The car was an old wreck. The roads were in terrible condition after years of war. And travel at night was unsafe because bandits infested isolated areas. One area about halfway between Genoa and Spezia was so dangerous that the Italian police regularly formed cars and trucks into convoys and escorted them through it with armored vehicles.

It was too late to join a convoy, but Father Alvaro was unwilling to wait until the next day, so the group set out. They got through the most dangerous area without incident but then began to suffer a series of flat tires. After the jack broke, they were forced to spend the rest of the night sleeping in the car. The next morning they learned that less than a mile away, bandits had assaulted a truck, tied the driver to a tree, and made off with the vehicle. Despite the urgency of reaching Rome, they stopped in Pisa for del Portillo to celebrate Mass, then pushed on. They had hoped to reach Rome in the early morning of the 27th, but they did not arrive until shortly after midnight.

The next day, immediately after celebrating Mass, del Portillo set out to visit cardinals. Three newly created Spanish cardinals were staying at the Spanish College, but officials there told him they were leaving the next day and had no time for seeing anyone. Del Portillo kept insisting and finally managed to see two of them, who signed previously prepared letters of recommendation. That same morning, he also visited the cardinal archbishop of Lisbon, who had met Escrivá and was happy to provide a recommendation. He suggested contacting the newly created cardinal of Lorenzo Marquez in the Portuguese colony of Mozambique, who agreed to see Escrivá in Madrid and eventually wrote a letter of recommendation. A few days later, del Portillo managed to meet Cardinal Frings, the archbishop of Cologne, to whom he explained Opus Dei in Latin since they had no other common language. Cardinal Frings was so taken with what he heard and with the personality of the young priest that he agreed to write the recommendation even though he had never before heard of Opus Dei.

Initial Negotiations in the Vatican

Armed with the letters of recommendation, Alvaro went to see officials in the Congregation for Religious. This was the office that would have to sign off on Opus Dei's request for pontifical status. The officials with whom del Portillo spoke agreed that it merited that status, and for a time it appeared papal approval would be granted quickly. Soon, however, difficulties began to appear. The original plan was for papal approval of Opus Dei without any change in its legal classification. But when Vatican officials looked more closely, they realized the Work did not fit into the category of a society of common life applied to it in 1943. Thus it could not simply be changed from a diocesan society to a pontifical one. It would need a new legal classification.

For more than a decade, the Holy See had been concerned with how various "new forms" of apostolate could fit into the legal structures in the 1917 Code of Canon Law. The undersecretary of the Congregation for Religious, Father Larraona, CMF, had been working for several years on new legislation and took the position that Opus Dei would have to wait for these new rules creating a legal category that suited it better. But the project had been proceeding very slowly and now seemed on hold. Approval apparently would be a long time coming.

Thanks to Msgr. Montini, del Portillo was received by Pope Pius XII on April 3. Recalling Alvaro's earlier visit in dress uniform, the Pope received him warmly and repeatedly expressed admiration for the apostolic work of Opus Dei. During their conversation, del Portillo had what he described to Escrivá as "the unheard-of nerve" to comment that it was a shame the decree on the new forms of apostolate had not yet come out. A few days later, the Pope told the head of the Congregation for Religious he wanted the new legislation issued as soon as possible.

In the following weeks, del Portillo did all he could to speed up the decree's approval, working closely with Father Larraona. But things still moved very slowly. On June 8, the experts of the Congregation for Religious voted that a "decree of praise" transforming Opus Dei into a papal institution should be approved, but only after the legislation governing the new forms of apostolate was completed.

Prospects for prompt approval looked bleak. Influential people in the Congregation for Religious thought the necessary new legislation would require amending the 1917 Code of Canon Law, an arduous process most people in the Vatican considered premature at best. Others opposed the new legislation on grounds that it posed a threat to the religious orders which had served the Church so well for many centuries. Father Larraona was in favor of the new legislation, but he saw nothing urgent about finishing it. He had much else to do and no qualms about setting aside his work on new forms of apostolate.

Summoning Escrivá to Rome

In early June, del Portillo concluded that there was little more he could do to speed up the process. He was acutely aware of the founder's serious health problems, but after careful consideration in prayer, he reluctantly decided that it was vital for the future of Opus Dei that Escrivá come to Rome promptly, and he wrote asking him to come. Del Portillo traveled to Genoa to meet Escrivá at the dock. The ship had run into a major storm and did not arrive until 11:00 p.m. on June 22. Restaurants were closed at that hour, so Alvaro was reduced to offering the founder a piece of Parmesan cheese he had saved in his pocket at lunch time. They spent the night in a modest hotel and set out by car for Rome. When they sighted the cupola of St. Peter's around 9:30 p.m., Escrivá prayed the Creed aloud.

The members of Opus Dei in Rome had rented an apartment in Piazza della Città Leonina, just across the street from the Vatican wall. The top floor apartment had two bedrooms, but they had converted one into an oratory. Five people—now, with Escrivá's arrival, six—crowded into these small quarters. The founder had a normal bed, but four of them rolled out thin mattresses on the floor each evening, while del Portillo set up a cot in the hallway.

Upon arriving, Escrivá was exhausted from the trip, but when he discovered that the apartment's terrace had an unimpeded view of the windows of the papal apartments, he spent the entire night there praying for the Holy Father. Del Portillo, moved by this display of affection for the Pope, told a friend in the secretary of state's office. Three or four days later, he discovered that everyone in the Vatican was laughing at the founder. "Those Spaniards are fanatics," they said.

Father Alvaro asked Msgr. Montini if he could get a photograph of Pope Pius XII for Escrivá, and a few days later he was able to give him a signed photo of the Holy Father inscribed to "our beloved son Josemaría Escrivá de Balaguer, founder of the Priestly Society of the Holy Cross and Opus Dei with a special blessing."

Further Negotiations

The weeks that followed were filled with visits to Vatican officials and work on the legislation concerning new forms of apostolate. Among those del Portillo met at this time was the future Cardinal Secretary of State Domenico Tardini, already a very influential person in the Vatican. Although Tardini was twenty-five years older than del Portillo, the two became close friends, and Tardini often invited him to say Mass at an orphanage he had founded.

Del Portillo spent many hours working with Father Larraona on the draft legislation, regularly inviting him for lunch followed by a working session in the afternoon. On several occasions, to get Father Larraona's complete attention and prevent him from being distracted with other matters, del Portillo and Escrivá took him to Fiuggi, a small resort town southeast of Rome, where they could work uninterruptedly for a few days at a time. Despite all their efforts, however, the project continued to move slowly.

Escrivá and del Portillo could not afford to remain indefinitely in Rome. The headquarters of Opus Dei was in Spain, and much work awaited them there. On the other hand, the people back in Spain who continued to criticize Opus Dei would be only too happy to see them return empty-handed. Perhaps for this reason, the head of the

Congregation for Religious arranged for them to receive two documents from the Holy See before leaving. The first, an apostolic brief entitled *Cum Societatis,* granted indulgences to the members of Opus Dei. The second, a letter from the congregation, praised the aims of Opus Dei. Neither affected the legal status of the Work, but these indications of Vatican approval would be helpful in fending off the attacks.

After Vatican officials returned from their summer vacations, del Portillo and Escrivá returned to Rome to continue their efforts. Yet it was obviously important that the secretary general be at Opus Dei headquarters in Madrid, especially when the founder was in Rome. This may be why Escrivá now named a new secretary general and appointed del Portillo procurator-general, charged with maintaining relations with the Holy See.

Once again del Portillo and Escrivá found their days filled with visits and drafting sessions. Many days they invited Father Larraona or other Vatican officials to lunch at the apartment in Città Leonina, although they had so little money that putting on a decent meal for a guest often meant eating little or nothing at other meals.

Father Alvaro visited Vatican officials time and again, showing no sign of tiredness or discouragement at their failure to understand exactly what he wanted or their unwillingness to grant it. His faith that Opus Dei was truly a work of God and what he was asking for was God's will gave him the patience and tenacity to persist. His successor, Bishop Echevarría, makes the point that this perseverance based on faith helped convince many high-ranking Vatican officials that he was concerned with carrying out God's will and not just getting his way.

Preliminary Papal Approval

Finally, on February 2, 1947, Pope Pius XII promulgated the apostolic constitution *Provida Mater Ecclesia*, establishing the legislative framework for what were called secular institutes. This cleared the way for the approval of Opus Dei as a secular institute of pontifical right on February 24, marking the close of an important chapter in which del Portillo played a vital role. His fervent prayer, his ability to make friends, his intelligence and diligence, and his complete identification with the mind of Escrivá were essential ingredients in the arduous process of winning papal approval.

The legal category of secular institute fit Opus Dei only imperfectly. The legislation on secular institutes was a compromise between the needs of Opus Dei, the desires of many other institutions, and the mentality of the personnel of the Congregation for Religious, many of whom understandably thought of secular institutes as a new type of religious order, with fewer restrictions than the traditional orders and congregations yet essentially similar. In many ways, the legislation represented an effort to adapt traditional religious life to the situation of people who felt called to carry out apostolate in the midst of the world. By contrast, the faithful of Opus Dei were not called to live in the world as an apostolic tactic but because they were ordinary faithful and citizens, men and women of the world. Still, despite its limitations, the new legislation gave Opus Dei a place in the universal Church and opened the way for its expansion to many countries.

Final Papal Approval

Partly to underline the secular character of the Work, del Portillo asked Msgr. Montini if he could arrange for Escrivá to be named a monsignor, an honorary title granted only to members of the secular clergy, never to members of religious orders. When the founder learned he had been given this honor, he wanted to reject it, but del Portillo convinced him to accept, arguing that his being a monsignor would help make clear the secular nature of the Work since only secular priests can be monsignors.

Del Portillo and Escrivá hoped papal approval would finally put an end to attacks on Opus Dei from within the Church, but that did not happen. Critics took advantage of the fact that its approval was preliminary to suggest that the Vatican did not really understand what Opus Dei was and, once it got to know it better, the approval would be withdrawn.[1] Escrivá, therefore, was anxious to obtain final approval as soon as possible. Del Portillo worked closely with him on preparing the necessary documents and explaining to Vatican officials the need for final approval soon after the granting of preliminary approval.

While the required documents were being prepared, Escrivá solved a troubling problem that must have been a cause of great suffering for del Portillo. The founder, a diocesan priest, felt that Our Lord was calling him to work closely with his brother diocesan priests to help them in their spiritual lives. Clearly they could benefit from living the spirit of Opus Dei: sanctifying their work as priests, sanctifying themselves in that work, and sanctifying others through it, just as the lay members of Opus Dei tried to do with their professional work.

For a long time, though, Escrivá could not see how diocesan priests could be members of the Work without creating

---

1. The Church's approval of a new institution is often a two-step process: preliminary approval and later, after more experience with the institution, final or definitive approval. Considering that Opus Dei was the first institution to be approved under the new legislation for secular institutes, it is no surprise that the approval granted in 1947 was preliminary.

a tension with the obedience they owed to their bishop. He had therefore reached the painful conclusion that God was asking him to leave Opus Dei to found a new institution for diocesan priests. He had talked about this with del Portillo, indicating that he would take over the leadership of Opus Dei. He even had a photograph taken showing a cupped pair of hands into which another hand was placing small donkeys: the cupped hands were del Portillo's, the hand placing the donkeys, which represented the members of Opus Dei, were Escrivá's.

In view of his extraordinarily strong sense of the special role of the founder, del Portillo must have found it very hard to think he would soon be asked to take his place. Fortunately, during the final stages of preparation for the definitive approval of Opus Dei, Escrivá found another solution to the problem: diocesan priests could belong to the Priestly Society of the Holy Cross. They would not owe obedience to the directors of Opus Dei, but only to their own bishops. Not only would there be no tension with their duties to their bishop, their connection with him would be strengthened by a spirituality that stressed the importance of unity with the bishop.

The Holy See definitively approved Opus Dei on June 16, 1950, with a decree entitled *Primum Inter* that underlined the secular character of the vocation to the Work and of its apostolates. The new legislation made it possible for diocesan priests to join the Priestly Society of the Holy Cross. It also opened the door for married people to belong to Opus Dei. The Work's legal status as a secular institute remained an imperfect solution, but here was another important step forward.

Serious New Threats

Less than a year later, Opus Dei once again found itself under attack. A number of young Italians had recently joined the Work, and a priest who ran a youth organization to which some of them had belonged exploited their parents' concerns for their children's future to get them to sign a letter to the Pope complaining that Opus Dei was destroying the lives of their loved ones. This attack directly affected del Portillo, who was at the time the head of Opus Dei's apostolic activities in Italy.

The letter could have had serious repercussions, since some of the people involved had good contacts at the highest levels of the Vatican. When Escrivá learned of it, his reaction was to turn to prayer and ask the members of the Work to be silent, to pray, to smile, and to continue working and studying. On May 14, 1951, accompanied by del Portillo, he consecrated the families of the members of Opus Dei to the Holy Family. One of the five families involved had already retracted its complaint, and the rest soon came to recognize that their concerns were unfounded.

About this same time, however, the founder began to sense that something else was wrong, though he did not know what. From time to time, he heard critical comments from members of the curia. Occasionally high-ranking churchmen gave him a cold shoulder or even denied that they were his friends.

The external events alone might not have overly troubled him, but, as del Portillo notes, the founder felt "a great uneasiness, an interior disquiet, because our Lord let him sense that some terrible plot was being hatched against the Work." Don Alvaro tried to cheer him up, pointing out that there were many vocations to Opus Dei and the members were living its spirit very well. The founder, however, continued to sense that something was wrong, and del Portillo inwardly shared his suffering. Once again Escrivá turned to the Blessed Virgin. On August 14, 1951, del Portillo went with him and two other members on a trip to Loreto, where tradition has it that the home of the Holy Family is preserved in a basilica. The next day, the feast of the Assumption, while del Portillo celebrated Mass, the founder consecrated Opus Dei to the Most Sweet Heart of Mary. In the following months, del Portillo accompanied Escrivá on pilgrimages to several shrines of Our Lady in Italy as well as to Lourdes, Fatima, and Saragossa.

In early January 1952 del Portillo, as procurator general of Opus Dei, received an official request from the Congregation for Religious for copies of the constitutions of Opus Dei and other documents. Since the Holy See already had these documents, the request for copies signaled some sort of official investigation. But the secrecy then prevailing in the Vatican meant they were neither told what was going on nor given an opportunity to defend themselves.

In mid-February, Cardinal Schuster of Milan advised the founder to recall what had happened to his fellow countryman, St. Joseph of Calasanz,[2] and to act in its light. Considering this warning in the context of the request for documents, it became clear that the plot against Opus Dei involved removing the founder as its head and separating the men's branch from the women's branch.

Del Portillo now insisted on cosigning a letter of protest to Cardinal Tedeschini, a personal friend who had recently been appointed cardinal protector of Opus Dei. Escrivá attempted to dissuade del Portillo from signing on

---

2. St. Joseph (1556–1648) founded an order called the Clerks Regular of the Religious Schools but was forced out of office as superior general through the scheming of some members and eventually had to see the order itself suppressed. It was restored after his death. St. Joseph was canonized in 1767.

the grounds that if he were eventually expelled, del Portillo would have to succeed him. But Alvaro did not yield. "No, Father. The Father's fate will be mine, whatever it is." He accompanied Escrivá to hand the letter personally to Cardinal Tedeschini, who a few days later read it to the Pope. Pius XII, who had not been informed about the machinations, immediately put a stop to them.

Thanks in no small part to del Portillo's loyalty and fervent prayer, a serious danger had been averted. But Opus Dei desperately needed peace to carry on its apostolic mission. Once again, Escrivá turned to prayer. On October 26, 1952, he consecrated Opus Dei to the Sacred Heart of Jesus. "Most Sacred Heart of Jesus, grant us peace!" he prayed incessantly. On an earlier occasion, after they had made their mental prayer together, Escrivá asked del Portillo what he had prayed about that day. He responded, "I repeated what I always do, but as if it were the first time. I said to him, 'I ask you for what the Father is asking you for.'" During this consecration to the Sacred Heart and throughout this whole difficult period, it is easy to imagine del Portillo praying this same prayer many times.

CHAPTER 11

BUILDING OPUS DEI
IN AND FROM ROME

Escrivá had written in *The Way*, "Catholic, apostolic, Roman! I want you to be very Roman." That desire extended not only to individuals; he was eager to "Romanize" Opus Dei as a whole. That involved, among other things, transferring its headquarters from Madrid to Rome and having members study in Rome, where they would grow in love for the Holy Father and the universal Church. But neither step could be taken while Opus Dei's only presence in the city was a small apartment. From the moment Escrivá arrived in Rome, both Msgr. Montini and Msgr. Tardini encouraged him to begin looking for property. "Even if you do miracles outside of Rome," Montini told him, "if those miracles aren't seen here, they don't count."

Roman real estate was a buyer's market at the time. Italy was still suffering from the devastation of the Second World War, and many large houses were available for a small fraction of what they would cost a few years later. The problem was that Opus Dei had almost no resources. Almost all of its 300 or so members were young, many still in college. The vast majority of them were in Spain. Although that country had avoided involvement in the Second World War, it was relatively undeveloped and still struggling to recover from the Civil War. All this meant Opus Dei had almost no money and very little prospect of getting any soon.

To most people, this would have suggested purchasing something small, with the hope of being able to acquire a larger house at some future date. But Escrivá and del Portillo were men of great vision and undaunted faith that God would provide. They fixed their sights on large houses with grounds on which more buildings could be constructed.

Villa Tevere

Early in 1947, del Portillo met the owner of a substantial Florentine-style villa with a one-acre garden that occupied much of an irregularly shaped block in the Parioli neighborhood. Parioli had a number of villas with large gardens and was beginning to be developed with luxury apartment buildings. On their first visit, in early February 1947, Escrivá and del Portillo were certain that they had found what they were looking for. During the next month, del Portillo conducted intensive negotiations with the owner and succeeded in bargaining down the asking price to the point that, as he would say many years later, "it seemed a gift."

No matter how good a buy, they were living crammed into a tiny apartment and had so little money that serving a decent meal to guests meant going hungry at other meals—and they did not have even a small fraction of the purchase price. The problem was complicated by the primitive structure of credit in Italy at the time. Mortgages were available only to the person who held title to a property, and sellers were naturally unwilling to transfer title before they got their money or had ironclad guarantees of getting it.

Over the course of a month of negotiations, however, the owner came to have such confidence in del Portillo that he agreed to transfer title on the basis of a symbolic down payment made up of American five- and ten-dollar gold pieces given to Escrivá that were being saved to make two chalices. Because the coins were destined to be melted down to make sacred vessels, the sales contract stipulated that they would be returned when payment was made. Payment of the full purchase price would be due in two months and depended on convincing a bank to give a mortgage for a high percentage of the total price despite Opus Dei owning no other property in Italy and having no reliable source of income.

At one point in the negotiations, another obstacle appeared: The owner insisted on payment in Swiss francs. When del Portillo told the founder, he was completely untroubled. "That's no problem at all. We have neither liras nor francs, and for Our Lord one currency is the same as the other." Eventually, after much prayer and a great deal of hard work, del Portillo managed to close the deal.

Occupying the Villa

They took possession of the property, which they called Villa Tevere, in July 1947 but could not get the tenants out of the villa. They could occupy only a small structure divided into two residences, one of which had served as the gatekeeper's house. The property had been leased to the government of Hungary and used as its embassy to the Holy See. Diplomatic relations between Hungary and the Vatican had been broken off, but a former embassy employee continued living in the villa and refused to move, in large part because he had no place else to go.

Although the Holy See was reluctant to acknowledge publicly that it no longer had diplomatic relations with a country with a large Catholic population, del Portillo was soon able to obtain such a declaration thanks to his friendship with Msgr. Tardini, the Vatican deputy secretary of state. This cleared the way for legal action against the abusive tenant.

Immediately after obtaining the declaration in August, del Portillo had the locks on the door of the villa changed. This moved the tenant to send a message threatening to shoot anyone who made further efforts to dislodge him. Del Portillo responded, saying he would have the gates to the entire property locked every night at 11 p.m. and would accept no further messages. If the former employee had anything to say, he could call personally, and del Portillo would decide whether to talk with him or not. At that point, the tenant backed down and negotiations became more civil.

In January 1948, the Hungarian agreed to move out, and del Portillo agreed to allow him to remain until he could find new accommodations. That took a year, but he finally vacated the villa on February 5, 1949. The founder, del Portillo, and other members of the Work moved in the next day.

Life in Il Pensionato

During the year and a half before they moved into the villa, they were extremely cramped living in the building they called *Il Pensionato* (the Hostel). Their living quarters consisted of a small living room, an oratory, a dining room, and two bedrooms. Escrivá had a poorly ventilated, humid room with the only normal bed in the house, but when someone fell sick he moved out and slept on the floor, often under the dining room table. Five people jammed into the only other bedroom, where they set up folding beds. Others slept in the hall. Del Portillo set up a folding bed each night in a small reception room next to the door and had to get up early in the morning because deliveries of bread and other staples came in that way.

In addition to housing the members of Opus Dei in Rome, *Il Pensionato* served as base for apostolic activities. Many young men came there for meditations, classes of Christian formation, and meetings with friends who lived there. In fall 1948 this already overcrowded house saw seven students arrive to study at Opus Dei's fledgling international center of studies, the Roman College of the Holy Cross. It had no space for a library, and the students sat on the stairs to study.

Money was in such short supply that for two or three years they could not turn on the heat. On an average day in January, the temperature in Rome reaches a high of 55 degrees and drops to 37 degrees at night. An unheated house soon becomes bone-chilling. Escrivá developed partial facial paralysis from the cold, and del Portillo suffered an attack of tonsillitis.

Remodeling and New Construction

Despite the lack of money, architects among the members of Opus Dei spent the year and a half it took to get possession of the villa preparing plans for major additions, including several stories on top and several other stories below ground. In addition, they developed initial plans for half a dozen new buildings, two large interior courtyards, and a number of smaller courtyards that would occupy most of the garden and surround the villa.

Construction began in July 1949 and would continue until January 1960. For a decade, del Portillo bore the crushing burden of finding money both for construction and to cover living and operating expenses. At first, to save money they hired a small contractor who required them to take responsibility for paying the workers directly every week. Compared to having a major general contractor, this arrangement saved some money, but it meant they lacked the financial cushion a large contractor would provide. Payments had to be made as work was done and materials were delivered. Expenses were running approximately 3 million lira a week, about $50,000 in 2013 US dollars.

The responsibility for paying the workers every week weighed heavily on del Portillo; he realized that "to fail to pay them one week would leave their entire family without food." Even in these desperate circumstances, he gave generous tips to workmen who worked especially well or went beyond the call of duty, and he made special payments to workers who found themselves facing an emergency. He also went out of his way to treat both workmen and suppliers with great refinement and charity, even when they pressed their demands rudely. On one occasion, when a furniture maker mistakenly made several extra kneelers, the person in charge of paying the bill suggested not paying for them, but del Portillo insisted that the entire bill be paid. "Don't be stingy," he said.

Along with bills for the construction, bills came pouring in for food, utilities, and other living expenses. In April 1954 they were so far behind in paying the gas bill that the company sent someone to collect the arrears or cut off the gas then and there. When the collector arrived at 11:00 a.m., there was no money in the house. He agreed to come back at 1:00 p.m., but made it clear that there would be no further extensions. Just a few minutes before 1:00, del Portillo arrived with the money.

"How did we pay?" he mused years later. "Our Lord made it possible for us to make it with loans and balancing acts. We robbed Peter to pay Paul. It was really crazy, and the cause of a lot of suffering. It was a miracle. I don't know how we did it, but somehow or another we always did pay."

Undoubtedly God did help them, but much also was due to del Portillo's efforts. In 1949, he made three trips to Spain to look for money. Both there and in Rome, he solicited donations and loans from friends, and asked them to cosign on mortgages, commercial loans, and letters of credit. He inspired such confidence in banks and other lending institutions that they extended loans to him despite the riskiness of the project. Once, when a large note was coming due, del Portillo tried several times to get the lender to roll it over, but with no success. Escrivá asked him to try one more time. The founder and several older members of the Work gathered in the oratory to pray for the results. When del Portillo returned, the broad smile on his face showed that he had succeeded. When asked, "How did you do it?" he responded simply, "I obeyed."

Many times, as the end of the week drew approached with nowhere near enough money in hand to pay the workers, del Portillo had to pound the streets looking for cash—despite running a fever that should have kept him in bed. A member of the Work who accompanied him on one such expedition was amazed that "he didn't comment at all on the effort involved; instead he maintained "his habitual smile and peace full of simplicity, just as if it were the most natural thing in the world. I recalled what our Father repeated so frequently—that ours should be a smiling asceticism." On one such occasion, Escrivá commented to two members, "All of my children in the Work are very holy, but between the holiest of them and Don Alvaro there is a great distance."

Through all this del Portillo maintained his good humor. When his closest collaborator on financing the construction worried aloud that they might end up in jail, he merely replied, "If that happens, be sure to bring me a typewriter and lots of paper." When Escrivá made a similar comment, del Portillo reassured him, "Don't worry, Father. Given the quantities involved, the more debts we have, the more credit they will extend us." Despite the good humor with which he faced these difficulties, the stress took its toll on him, leading to frequent high fevers, cramps, and vomiting.

Not until 1955, almost six years after the project began, were they able to engage a major general contractor. This did not reduce the amount that had to be paid, but it did give them some breathing room.

The results of del Portillo's magnanimity can be seen today in the complex of buildings that is Villa Tevere. Finished in 1960, it comprises some 150,000 square feet. The buildings were built to last for centuries, without skimping. The twenty-two oratories in particular reflect in their generous dimensions and exquisite decoration a love of God that did not shrink in the face of sacrifices. Most people confronting the almost impossible challenges of this project would have settled for much less. Del Portillo seems never to have wavered in his commitment to provide the headquarters Opus Dei needed for the future, no matter the cost to himself.

Rector of the Roman College of the Holy Cross

With Vatican approval, world peace, and a growing number of vocations, Opus Dei was poised to spread its message to new countries and new continents. This called for in-depth formation: philosophy and theology along with a thorough grounding in the spirit of Opus Dei and how to live it. For this, daily direct contact with the founder was the best form of instruction. And if he was going to live in Rome, this meant creating an international center of formation there.

On June 29, 1948, Escrivá established the Roman College of the Holy Cross. He asked Father Alvaro to serve as rector. The first year there were only seven students. But even though the numbers were so small, this new task involved a great deal of work for del Portillo—devising the curriculum, training the staff, and above all seeing to the personal formation of the students, many of whom were to play a vital role in Opus Dei's expansion, either as priests or directors.

One early student of the Roman College vividly recalls the time he spent in Rome with del Portillo. "Whenever he ran into one of us, he always had a smile, the authentic expression of his profound brotherly affection. During the years I spent with him, he reprimanded me several times about things required by our vocation. . . . He corrected us whenever necessary without letting defects slip by, but without losing supernatural outlook or affection. When he corrected you, you understood clearly what needed to be changed, but at the same time you felt content and grateful."

Under del Portillo's leadership, the Roman College grew rapidly from the initial seven students: fourteen the following year, twenty the year after that, and 123 in 1954 when he stepped down as rector, having reached the goal of 120 the founder had set. Crowding persisted, and money was so short that students walked a considerable distance to and from classes in the Roman universities to save the miniscule bus fare. The smokers among them purchased a few cigarettes at a time, lacking money to buy a full pack. On several occasions, donors gave money for a piano, but the money ended up going for food. "We have eaten several pianos," Escrivá commented with amusement.

Clearly the students needed a place where they could escape the brutal heat of Rome during the summer, but that seemed out of the question. When del Portillo told the founder about a large agricultural property that he might be able to purchase from a friend—near the town of Terracina, about halfway between Rome and Naples, with easy access to an unspoiled beach—Escrivá responded, "But, my son, we can't even eat!" Del Portillo insisted: "Father, we could at least try. The boys need a place to take it easy during the summer. Without one they will get sick."

Thanks to del Portillo's friendship with the owner and to imaginative planning, they were able to acquire the 3,000-acre farm in late 1951. Del Portillo devised a financing scheme that permitted the almost 300 peasants who had been employed as laborers on the farm to acquire their own parcels of land. In addition, he arranged for them to be able to learn about the faith and improve their formation. The Vatican newspaper described the operation as "a vast program of social and apostolic activities . . . an agrarian reform carried out with a Catholic spirit."

The Work retained a small fraction of the property. For many years it was used as a farm, providing vegetables, milk, meat, and other products for the growing number of people living in Villa Tevere, while also serving for more than fifteen years as a summer place for the students of the Roman College. Living conditions were very primitive at the start, and classes were held in the open air. Since there was no money to buy desks or chairs, an ingenious student suggested digging shallow circular pits, about two feet deep and twenty-five feet in diameter, where students could sit on the ground but lean back against the earth wall during classes.

Even with primitive conditions, escaping from Rome in the summer and having easy access to the Mediterranean was a great improvement over summer in Rome. Nevertheless, until 1957 del Portillo and Escrivá continued to remain in the city all summer, now and then visiting the students in Terracina but returning to Rome at night. When finally they were able to get away from Rome for part of the summer, del Portillo concentrated on helping the founder rest rather than doing things he personally enjoyed.

Laying the Foundations of Opus Dei in Italy

Despite the urgency of obtaining papal approval for Opus Dei and the overwhelming amount of work facing him from the moment he arrived back in Rome in 1946, del Portillo found time to take spiritual care of the two members of the Work who had been living in Italy for several years and helping out with their apostolate.

The first person to join Opus Dei in Italy was a Croatian refugee, Vladimir Vince, who had been the assistant to Anton Wurster, the representative to the Holy See of the independent Croatia created by the German dismemberment of Yugoslavia in 1941. After Tito's reunification of Yugoslavia in 1943, the two no longer had diplomatic immunity and feared arrest by the Nazis who controlled Rome at the time. They were forced to seek asylum, first in a convent and then in a monastery. After emerging from hiding, they met José Orlandis and Salvador Canals, members of the Work studying in Rome. Shortly after meeting del Portillo, Vladimir joined Opus Dei in April 1946.[1]

In a letter to Escrivá, Vladimir spoke of the importance of del Portillo's role in his vocation: "Don Alvaro is a marvelous help for me. He solves all my difficulties. If at times I don't manage to explain clearly to him what is happening to me, he reads my thoughts and understands me."

The move from Cittá Leonina to *Il Pensionato* opened the doors to a broader apostolate with young Italians. Del Portillo threw himself into the task, preaching meditations and days of recollection, hearing confessions, and giving spiritual direction. He refused to allow illness to slow him down. One day, when several young visitors had come to *Il Pensionato*, he got up at 6:00 a.m. to say Mass for them despite being sick and suffering from dizziness.

---

1. Anton Wuster joined Opus Dei several years later in Spain.

In November 1947, Francesco Angelicchio became the first Italian member of Opus Dei. During the next three months, three other young Italians joined the Work. During 1948, del Portillo accompanied the founder on several trips to prepare for future apostolic activities in the north and south of Italy. In October 1948 Escrivá created an Italian region within Opus Dei and named del Portillo its "counselor," or head. He continued to serve as the head of Opus Dei's activities in Italy until 1951.

Not content with trying to expand Opus Dei's apostolic activities in Rome, del Portillo encouraged the young men who had recently joined the Work to travel on weekends to other cities, and he joined them on the trips. In the first year they visited at least nine cities, where they met with friends and acquaintances, gave classes of Christian formation, explained the spirit of Opus Dei, and encouraged those who attended the classes to invite others. By late 1949, they were able to open small centers in Milan and Palermo. Years later, someone asked del Portillo how they could do so much with no money and very few people. With a look of perplexity prompted by the question, he replied, "When you work for our Lord, he takes care of providing what is needed."

The growth of Opus Dei's apostolate in Italy created a need for a conference center for retreats, workshops, and other formational activities. Del Portillo had preached a retreat in May 1948 in a large, rundown house in Castelgandolfo, the hill town south of Rome on the shores of Lake Albano where the popes had their summer residence. An elderly countess he had met a short time before had a lease on the building, which belonged to the Holy See. In the months that followed, Alvaro occasionally took Escrivá to walk along the shore of Lake Albano to get the exercise the founder's doctor had prescribed. As they walked, they frequently offered prayers that they would be able to acquire the house as a conference center—more complicated than it might seem since the land on which the house stood belonged to the Holy See.

The following year, the countess gave up her rights to the building, and Pope Pius XII gave Opus Dei the right to use it. Given the precarious state of Opus Dei's finances, the costs of remodeling and maintenance meant a significant additional burden for del Portillo. Immediately after taking possession of the house, which they called Villa delle Rose, they began there a course of theology for members of the Work. During more than a month, del Portillo and the founder drove back and forth daily from Rome to give talks and classes about the spirit of Opus Dei and to speak personally with the participants in the course.

By summer 1950, apostolic activities in Rome had grown so much that a separate house was needed. The young Italian members of the Work found a freestanding house about halfway between Villa Tevere and the Vatican which could serve the purpose well. But by the day before they were scheduled to meet with the owner, they had managed to put together only a small fraction of the sum needed to buy the property. So they went to del Portillo, who said, "You have done everything you could. Our Lord will do the rest. Go and pray." The next day, an anonymous benefactor sent Escrivá the necessary funds. Today the house is still a center of Opus Dei.

Studies and Working in the Vatican

Del Portillo's work as Escrivá's principal assistant, procurator general of Opus Dei, rector of the Roman College of the Holy Cross, and head of Opus Dei in Italy added up to an overwhelming load. Even so, he found time also to earn a doctorate in canon law and to work in the Vatican.

During the academic year 1946–47, he enrolled in the canon law program at the Lateran Pontifical Athenaeum. The year after, he transferred to the Angelicum Pontifical Athenaeum. In June 1949 he earned a doctorate summa cum laude with a dissertation on secular institutes. One of his professors publicly described him as the best student he had ever had. Not content with earning his degree, del Portillo continued to study and write, publishing three scholarly articles between 1955 and 1959.

For two-and-a-half years after the promulgation of the legislation on secular institutes, Don Alvaro served as secretary of the commission of the Congregation for Religious charged with implementing the legislation. These duties took up his mornings most days. Even after he resigned that position, he still spent most of his mornings in the Vatican working on projects for the Holy See. This gave him, he told his mother in a letter written on the occasion of his fortieth birthday, "the joy of doing my bit in things that affect the universal Church at its center, which is the Holy See."

Some days, Escrivá went to the Vatican to meet del Portillo as he left his office and walk home with him. During the three-mile walk, they prayed the Rosary and talked about the work the founder had done that morning, the projects awaiting them that afternoon, and plans for developing the apostolates of Opus Dei. (Del Portillo's work in the Vatican was put off limits by official secrecy, so they could not talk about that.)

Once Again Secretary General

In August 1956, Opus Dei held its second general congress in Einsiedeln, a small town in Switzerland with an important shrine of the Blessed Virgin Mary. The congress decided to transfer the headquarters of Opus Dei's men's branch to

Rome, where the headquarters of the women's branch had been located since 1953. It again named del Portillo secretary general, the position he would hold until becoming Escrivá's first successor in 1975.

At the 1956 congress, del Portillo was also named *custos*, or aide, of the head of Opus Dei—that is to say, one of the two people charged with accompanying the founder and helping him with spiritual and practical matters. In the spiritual realm, that made him officially responsible for giving Escrivá a kind of help he had given to him for many years, particularly since becoming his confessor.

During the congress, at a moment when del Portillo was not present, Escrivá commented that if anyone in Opus Dei could be considered his collaborator, it was Don Alvaro. He relied on del Portillo's advice in all areas and rarely decided anything important without consulting him. They thought so much alike that often just a few words were enough for them to understand each other.

From 1956 on, meetings of Opus Dei's regional directors were held frequently in Rome. Del Portillo played an important role in them, especially by emphasizing unity with the founder. One participant found that del Portillo's attitude of filial obedience, his availability for whatever he was asked to do, and his attentiveness to the founder were "a living lesson of the union we needed to live to make the apostolate fruitful all over the world."

In the 1950s and 1960s, the international governing bodies of both the men's and the women's branches of Opus Dei were largely composed of very young people, and membership turned over frequently. This was excellent experience for many people who would subsequently hold positions of responsibility in Opus Dei throughout the world, but it meant a great deal more work for del Portillo helping to train them. Escrivá was well aware of this. When he told a particularly young woman she had just been appointed procurator of the women's branch, he added, "Don't worry, my daughter. Don Alvaro will teach you everything." For his part, del Portillo told her, "There is only one condition for your being able to support the Father effectively, that you be humble."

In dealing as secretary general with the members of the international governing bodies, del Portillo avoided giving his own opinion, focusing on transmitting the founder's mind. Similarly, in giving meditations to members of the Work in Rome, he stressed fidelity to the founder, pointing out the privilege they enjoyed in learning the spirit of the Work directly from him and the responsibility that brought with it.

Along with his regular work, del Portillo continued to be the person to whom Escrivá turned for solving especially difficult problems. As Opus Dei was getting started in Ireland, for instance, the archbishop of Dublin refused to grant permission to open a center there, even though the request was backed by the papal representative in Ireland. Three different times, three different priests of Opus Dei visited the archbishop, but to no avail. Finally Escrivá asked del Portillo to go to Ireland and try to solve the problem. Del Portillo had no new arguments to offer, but his warmth and simplicity won over the archbishop, who not only granted the necessary permission but invited him to join him for dinner, something he rarely did.

Ill Health

In the sixteen years between his move to Rome in 1946 and the beginning of the Second Vatican Council, del Portillo accomplished a quantity of work that would have impressive for a man in good health. He, in fact, was in poor health

much of the time. He had a chronic liver condition, perhaps traceable to privations suffered during the Civil War,
especially ill-treatment in prison. This led, as we have seen,
to frequent cramps, high fevers, nausea, and vomiting. He
also suffered from severe headaches, as well as toothaches
requiring repeated visits to the dentist. Excessive work, lack
of sleep, and stress were no doubt aggravating factors. The
person who kept the official diary of Villa Tevere observed
that his health problems were due to "too much work and
concern for everyone and everything except himself."

Besides chronic illness, Alvaro suffered several serious
health crises. In February 1950 he began to experience severe
intestinal pain. As usual, his first response was to attach little
importance to it and continue working. After several days
the founder insisted that he see a doctor, and he was diagnosed with appendicitis and sent to a clinic for surgery. Seeing him in pain, Escrivá improvised a little dance to make
him laugh and take his mind off the pain.

The surgery uncovered such extensive adhesions and
necrosis that the surgeon concluded nothing could be done
and began to close up the incision, but del Portillo's personal physician, Dr. Faelli, who was in the operating room,
intervened. "This man is my brother, so you have to do
whatever is necessary to save him." The operation was
successful but took much longer than expected, and con-
sequently del Portillo was a long time coming out of the
anesthesia. He failed to respond when his name was called
loudly, but when Escrivá said to him in a normal tone of
voice, "Alvaro, my son!" he immediately opened his eyes.
The founder later commented, "Alvaro obeys, even when he
is under anesthesia." Recovery was difficult, and at times del
Portillo was delirious. In his delirium he repeated, "I want
to work alongside the Father, with all my strength, till the
end of my life."

In 1959, Don Alvaro suffered another crisis—a prostate abscess requiring surgery. Again recovery was very slow, and he remained hospitalized for more than a month.

Del Portillo saw in illness an opportunity to draw closer to God. "The Lord knows what we are like," he said, "and therefore he sends us from time to time an illness to bring us closer to him. If sickness is borne well, it unites us to God and is a treasure." He bore it with cheerfulness, good humor, and a smile, with no interruption to his work except in extreme circumstances. Many days, when he could hardly have been blamed for staying in bed, he kept working as if nothing were wrong, giving no sign of his pain, smiling, and taking an interest in others.

Deaths in the Family

The 1950s brought the deaths of two people whose passing was particularly painful to del Portillo: his mother and Escrivá's sister, Carmen. Clementina del Portillo died suddenly on March 10, 1955, in Madrid. She was attending a retreat in a church near her home and had just come home from Mass when she suffered a massive cerebral hemorrhage; she died that evening. The Spanish custom of burial shortly after death and the time it still took in 1955 to get from Rome to Madrid made it impossible for Don Alvaro to attend the funeral. Speaking of the Mass he celebrated for his mother upon learning of her death, he said in a letter to his brothers and sisters, "I have never prayed with greater devotion, and the words of the liturgy, *vita mutatur non tollitur* [life is changed not taken away] have never given me greater peace. The Lord gives me security that is almost more physical than moral now that Mama is already in heaven. This security brings with it a profound peace in the midst of pain . . . My sadness is great, not for Mama, but for me, for all the good I failed to do and for all the evil I may have done. For all of that I ask pardon from God, from Mama, and from you."

Alvaro had known Escrivá's sister Carmen since he joined Opus Dei in 1935. She played a vital role in the early development of Opus Dei, although never a member herself. She was living in Rome when she was diagnosed with terminal cancer in 1957. Escrivá, perhaps fearing his emotions would get the better of him, asked Alvaro to break the news to her. When, a few months later, it was time for Carmen to receive the anointing of the sick, Escrivá wanted to administer the sacrament but had barely begun when he was overcome by emotion and had to ask Don Alvaro to continue. When the ceremony was over, the founder turned to several women of Opus Dei who were present and asked their pardon for what he called his bad example. Del Portillo immediately intervened: "Father, you have always taught us that we have to have heart, and you have just demonstrated that you have it."

Escrivá's Cure

Don Alvaro played a leading role in a particularly dramatic moment in the founder's life. For years, del Portillo had given him an injection of insulin just before dinner. A new kind of long-acting insulin had recently been prescribed by the doctor. On April 27, 1954, shortly after sitting down to dinner, Escrivá suddenly said, "Alvaro, absolution!" Don Alvaro did not understand, and the founder repeated "absolution" twice before himself beginning to recite the formula of sacramental absolution. At that moment, he lost consciousness, turning a kind of reddish purple and then ashen yellow, while his body seemed to contract. Doctors later identified the crisis as an acute allergic reaction to the new insulin, but at the time del Portillo did not know what the problem was. He gave him absolution immediately, called the doctor, and, supposing that the problem was too much insulin, put sugar in Escrivá's mouth, forcing him to swallow it with water. By the time the doctor arrived, Escrivá had regained consciousness, but for several hours afterwards he could not see. When he could finally see himself in a mirror, he said, "Alvaro, my son, now I know how I'll look when I'm dead."

"You look fresh as a daisy, Father," Don Alvaro answered. "You should've seen yourself a few hours ago—you really did look like a corpse."

From that moment, Escrivá no longer suffered from diabetes. On doctor's advice, he stopped taking insulin, and for the rest of his life he no longer needed a diabetic diet, although some of the consequences of diabetes continued to plague him as long as he lived. His attending physician described his recovery as a "scientifically inexplicable cure."

CHAPTER 12

THE SECOND VATICAN COUNCIL

On January 25, 1959, St. John XXIII startled the Catholic world by announcing that he had decided to call an ecumenical council. It was almost a century since the close of the First Vatican Council (1869–70) and almost 500 years since the Council of Trent (1545–63). Preparation for the council was entrusted to a commission headed by Cardinal Tardini. All the bishops of the world were invited to suggest topics for discussion. Much of the early preparatory work was to be done by the Vatican departments, which naturally sought outside help to deal with the increased work load.

In his sixteen years in Rome, del Portillo had earned a reputation in the curia for intelligence, wisdom, love of the Church, diligence, an ability to get a great deal done in a short time, and excellent people skills. On May 2 he was named a consultor of the Sacred Congregation of the Council (now called the Congregation for the Clergy). In August he became president of the preparatory commission charged with developing materials on the laity and a member of the commission on modern methods of apostolate. The documents prepared by the preparatory commission on the laity stressed the universal call to holiness—that God calls all men and women, not just a select few, to holiness. This became a key element in the council's central doctrinal document, the Constitution on the Church, *Lumen Gentium*. It seems probable that del Portillo played a significant role in this development.

In the period just before the council opened on October 11, 1962, del Portillo was named an expert (*peritus*) and served in that capacity on three commissions. On November 8, 1962, he was named secretary of the Commission on the Discipline of the Clergy and the Christian People. This made him the second-ranking person in the commission whose president was Cardinal Ciriaci.

Directing the commission's work on a day-to-day basis and presiding over its meetings when the cardinal was absent posed formidable challenges. The members of the commission held sharply divided opinions. Some saw priests as primarily members of the hierarchy, others primarily as ministers. Some preferred to stress the priest's role in administering the Eucharist and the sacrament of penance; others stressed above all the ministry of the Word. The members of the commission included two cardinals in addition to Ciriaci, fifteen archbishops, thirteen bishops, and forty experts from sixteen different countries. Many members were men who had governed dioceses for years or held other responsible positions in the Church and were accustomed to getting their own way.

A canonist who worked with del Portillo a few years later on the Commission for the Reform of Canon Law described Alvaro's approach: "In meetings he followed discussions attentively, always trying to get to the bottom of the problem, and spoke only to make specific and very concise contributions. He did not make useless observations which would prolong meetings unnecessarily. These qualities of simplicity, depth, efficiency, cordiality, and respect account for the high esteem in which people held him and for the serious attention they paid to his opinions."

The work of the commission was difficult and at times frustrating. The preparatory committees had drafted three separate decrees dealing with different aspects of the life and ministry of priests. In early 1963 the group that directed the overall work of Vatican II decided that the three decrees should be combined in a single decree. It was not easy to reach consensus on which topics to cover and which to omit, but the commission succeeded in producing a draft. It had hardly done so, however, when, in November 1963, it was instructed to reduce the entire text to ten very short propositions. The council fathers debated them from October 13–15, 1964, found them insufficient, and rejected them.

Although drafting a new decree would mean much more work for him at a time when he was suffering from conjunctivitis and sinusitis, del Portillo suggested that the commission propose to the governing body of the council a new full-blown decree, taking into account what the council fathers said during the debate on the ten propositions. A week later the suggestion was accepted. Del Portillo reconvened the commission and informed the members that they needed to produce a new text, incorporating the many observations during the debate on the rejected propositions. It had to be finished in a few weeks to allow the bishops to take it home with them and study it before the next session.

The commission could make use of prior drafts, but reaching final agreement on a text was extremely demanding, especially in light of the very tight time constraints and the large number of comments to be considered. Many days they worked until after midnight, often in a residence where the council fathers and experts were living, since the Vatican offices were locked early in the evening.

Del Portillo's guidance of the work of the commission was later described by its president, Cardinal Ciriaci, as "wise, tenacious, and amiable." According to Cardinal Mayer, a German Benedictine, Don Alvaro displayed "a mind sincerely open to the new horizons that are constantly being opened in human thought, but completely removed from the ingenuous 'spirit of adventure' of some theologians who enjoyed great popularity in the media. . . . He saw the criterion for discovering the truth in the statement of Saint Vincent of Lerins that development in dogma involves preserving 'the same dogma, the same sense and the same meaning.'"

The president of the bishops' conference of Puerto Rico, looking back in 1994 on his participation in the Council, stressed the positive attitude Don Alvaro maintained even in the face of difficulties. "I always heard [from him]," he wrote, "words of understanding and excusing of others. . . . It was edifying to see how intransigent he was with regard to error, but, at the same time, how understanding with regard to persons. He could see a positive side to everything."

Cardinal Tedeschini, for his part, was impressed with the fortitude Don Alvaro displayed. "When it comes to defending the Church or the Work," he commented, "he defends it with the strength of a lion."

By the end of November 1964, the commission completed the draft of what would become the decree *Presbyterorum Ordinis*. At the start of the fourth and final session of the Council in fall 1965, a major difficulty threatened to arise. The draft addressed the question of priestly celibacy at some length. Some journalists, hoping for conflict on this subject, were gratified to learn from two bishops that they planned to speak against requiring celibacy. Hearing of this, del Portillo informed the secretary general of the council, who in turn informed Pope Paul VI, who had succeeded Pope John XXIII. Faced with the probability of tendentious

news coverage, the Pope asked the council fathers in a letter
to refrain from floor debate on the subject; he added that he
wanted to preserve in the Latin Church this ancient tradition reflecting the full consecration of priests to Christ and
their complete dedication to the service of the Church and
souls. When the letter was read aloud on October 11, the
vast majority of bishops broke into thunderous applause.
Although there was no floor debate on the subject, celibacy
was thoroughly explored in writing, with more than 1,000
bishops submitting more than 1,600 comments.

   Presbyterorum ordinis was approved by the council
fathers by a vote of 2,394 to four. It is divided into three
principal parts, which discuss the priesthood in the ministry
of the Church, the ministry of priests, and the life of priests.
This is not the place to explore the text of the decree, which
is readily available on the Vatican website, but one aspect
merits particular attention here. In order to meet pastoral
needs better, achieve a better distribution of priests, and provide priestly support for specific pastoral tasks, the decree
calls for the creation of more dynamic and flexible structures—international seminaries, special personal dioceses,
and personal prelatures. In addition to its possible significance in many other areas of the Church's life, the call for
personal prelatures opened the door to Opus Dei's eventually becoming one, thereby bringing to completion Escrivá's
lifelong quest for an adequate legal status for Opus Dei. It
is easy to imagine del Portillo's joy when the council voted
virtually unanimously in favor of the decree.

   The material which the Commission on the Discipline
of the Clergy and the Christian People received from the
preparatory commission already contained a reference to
prelatures without territory, another name for personal prelatures. It is very probable that Don Alvaro played a leading
role in presering this reference through the many drafts that

finally led up to the decree *Presbyterorum ordinis,* but determining the exact nature of that role would require a thorough study of the commission's work in this area. Personal prelatures were not without precedent, nor was del Portillo the only person involved in the drafting of *Presbyterorum ordinis* who might have been expected to back the idea. Bishop Marty, a member of the commission, was familiar with the prelature of Pontigni, better known as the Mission de France, that was in some ways a forerunner of personal prelatures. Other members of the commission may also have had an interest in the topic.

The presence in Rome of bishops and theologians from all over the world presented a unique opportunity to get to know many of them and tell them about Opus Dei. Despite the pressure of work, del Portillo spent many hours chatting informally with bishops, having lunch or a cup of coffee with them, and introducing them to Escrivá. He was almost always present when the founder entertained cardinals and bishops or went to visit them.

Many of the people he met during the council became lifelong friends. A prominent theologian who frequently attended international congresses once remarked that when he told new acquaintances he belonged to Opus Dei, the reply often was that they had a good friend in the Work— Alvaro del Portillo. Another indicator of the impression he made on people was that a number of bishops asked del Portillo to be their confessor while they were in Rome.

He was habitually open even to people who were critical of him and Opus Dei. One day he was introduced to the Swiss theologian Hans Küng, who had openly criticized Opus Dei in a meeting with council fathers and experts. Rather than simply shaking hands, del Portillo embraced him, saying, "As Christians and priests, we should love each other and pray for one another, all the more because we are both attempting to help the Vicar of Christ in the work of the Second Vatican Council." Although Küng did not accept the invitation, Don Alvaro offered to give him whatever information he might want about Opus Dei and introduce him to its founder.

Contacts with Pope Paul VI

Father Alvaro had two occasions to meet with Pope Paul VI during the council. One was an audience the Holy Father granted to Escrivá on January 24, 1964. At the end of the audience, he invited Father Alvaro, with whom he had been friends since 1946, to enter. Thinking of their many years of friendship, the Pope commented to del Portillo, "I have become old." To which Father Alvaro replied, "Your Holiness, you have become Peter." At the end of the audience, as photos were being taken, the Holy Father murmured softly to del Portillo, "Don Alvaro, Don Alvaro . . ."

On November 21, 1965, Pope Paul inaugurated the Centro ELIS, a major educational center for working class youth in a poor neighborhood on the outskirts of Rome. The center, entrusted to Opus Dei by St. John XXIII, included a technical school together with a residence, a library, a sports school, and a hospitality training center for young women. A large, newly constructed parish church entrusted to the priests of Opus Dei was immediately adjacent. The Pope had suggested holding the inauguration during one of the council sessions so that cardinals and bishops who were in Rome could attend. Many did. As he was leaving after dedicating the church and visiting the Centro ELIS, the Pope embraced Escrivá, commenting, "Here everything is Opus Dei." Del Portillo was overjoyed to hear the Holy Father express his appreciation for the work Opus Dei was doing there.

A Very Full Plate

Because of his duties as secretary general of Opus Dei, del Portillo had to turn down many opportunities to give lectures and to meet with groups of council fathers in contexts that would have made him more broadly known in ecclesiastical circles. Perhaps for this reason, his services during the council did not lead to promotions. The vast majority of the secretaries of commissions were named bishops shortly after the end of the council. Most went on to occupy prominent positions in the Vatican.

Del Portillo was not troubled at not receiving offers of prominent positions. In fact, he shunned opportunities to climb the ecclesiastical ladder. When a friend offered to propose him for an important position in the Congregation for the Clergy, he asked him not to do so, explaining that God's will for him was that he dedicate his life to helping the founder of Opus Dei. He was interested in doing God's will, not in having an ecclesiastical career.

Even though he turned down many speaking engagements and other invitations, he often managed to fulfill all his duties only by cutting back severely on sleep. As he said in a letter written in 1961 to a friend, "You say that I work a great deal, and it is true. I have to cut back more and more on sleep, but I'm happy to do it in order to fulfill the demands of my vocation."

What he did not cut down on was time dedicated directly to God. He celebrated Mass daily, spent an hour a day in mental prayer, said the Divine Office, and fulfilled the other practices of piety that formed part of the plan of life he had learned from Escrivá in the early days of his vocation. Rather than seeing the time dedicated to prayer as an obstacle to getting other things done, del Portillo found in prayer and a sense of God's presence the key to accomplishing all he had to do. Years later he explained,

"To multiply our time . . . we need to have more presence of God. Then we will work with greater peace and greater intensity and with more desire of doing things well. As a result, our time will be multiplied, because we do things better, with more interest, with a greater desire to get them right. That way we get distracted less and waste less time."

CHAPTER 13

THE POST-CONCILIAR
DECADE

During the ten years between the end of the council and
the death of Escrivá, del Portillo continued to work at
the founder's side as the secretary general of Opus Dei, his
confessor, and his most trusted collaborator and confidant.
He also continued to serve the universal Church. In 1964
he had been named a consultor of the Pontifical Commission for the Revision of the Code of Canon Law. This position would occupy a large part of his time for almost twenty
years until the new code was finally promulgated in 1983. In
1966 Pope Paul VI appointed him a consultor of the Congregation for the Doctrine of the Faith and a judge of its tribunal. Referring to Don Alvaro's work for the congregation,
Cardinal Ratzinger (later Pope Benedict XVI) wrote: "His
service . . . as consultor for many years was characterized
by his modesty and availability under all circumstances.
His competence and experience enriched in a singular way
the congregation."

Although del Portillo's life in the years following the
council was externally little different from what it had been
in the decade before the council, it was marked with special
joys and special sufferings. Observing the continuing growth
and development of Opus Dei was a continuing source of
joy. Despite the widespread dissent and conflict taking place

within the Church, Opus Dei remained closely united to the Holy Father and to its founder. The number of members continued to grow rapidly. Year after year, substantial groups of young men who had been formed in Rome at the founder's side were ordained priests of Opus Dei. During the decade 1965–1974, they numbered almost 400, while in those years the total membership of Opus Dei increased from some 33,000 to 60,000.

To provide an adequate site for the formation of the of young men who came to the Roman College of the Holy Cross each year from countries all around the world, the founder decided to build a new complex of buildings in the outskirts of Rome. Del Portillo enthusiastically supported this decision, although he was aware that it would involve much additional work for him and would seem unrealistic to many at a time when so many seminaries were closing.

Rejoicing in the Teachings of the Council

The results of the Second Vatican Council were another source of happiness. Del Portillo saw in the council's documents the Holy Spirit pouring out his light and grace on the Church. He rejoiced in many aspects of the council's teaching, especially at seeing many of the characteristic features of the spirit of Opus Dei proposed to the entire Church.

In the Dogmatic Constitution on the Church, *Lumen Gentium*, the council declared that "all the faithful of Christ of whatever rank or status are called to the fullness of the Christian life and to the perfection of charity," and that "all the faithful of Christ are invited to strive for the holiness and perfection of their own proper state." This had been a central feature of Opus Dei's message since 1928.

The same document painted a picture of the active role of the laity and the positive value of secularity; this was what del Portillo had heard from Escrivá from the beginning of his vocation. "What specifically characterizes the laity," the council taught, "is their secular nature. . . . The laity, by their very vocation, seek the kingdom of God by engaging in temporal affairs and by ordering them according to the plan of God. . . . [I]t is their special task to order and to throw light upon these affairs in such a way that they may come into being and then continually increase according to Christ to the praise of the Creator and the Redeemer."

The Decree on the Apostolate of the Laity, *Apostolicam Actuositatem*, stressed that Christ does not want his lay followers to be passive, but to contribute actively to the life of the Church: "The laity likewise share in the priestly, prophetic, and royal office of Christ and therefore have their own share in the mission of the whole people of God in the Church and in the world." They are called to spread the good news of Christ, the council taught, primarily in the setting of their ordinary lives: "Their temporal activity openly bears witness to Christ and promotes the salvation of men. Since the laity, in accordance with their state of life, live in the midst of the world and its concerns, they are called by God to exercise their apostolate in the world like leaven, with the ardor of the spirit of Christ."

These facets of the council's teaching, which explain Pope Francis' description of Escrivá as a "precursor" of the council, gave del Portillo a particularly deep joy.

Suffering with the Church

Father Alvaro's joy at the richness of the council's teaching did not prevent him from suffering intensely due to the Church's many problems in the years after Vatican II. The French Dominican theologian Yves Congar, whom St. John Paul II would name a cardinal, entitled his book about the situation of the Church in 1969 *In the Midst of the Thunderstorm.* Pope Paul VI lamented: "Through some crack, the smoke of Satan has entered the temple of God." He described the state of the Church as one of "doubt, uncertainty, puzzlement, disquiet, dissatisfaction, and confrontation." Instead of the sunshine hoped for after the council, the Church experienced, the Pope observed, "a day of clouds, of storms, of darkness, of searching, and of uncertainty." In the same vein, Escrivá frequently described the decade following the close of the council as a "time of trial" for the Church.

The history of the post-conciliar era is complex, but certain elements stand out. Some who applauded the Second Vatican Council as a revolutionary break with Church history rather than a development of Christian tradition openly denied key Catholic beliefs such as the real presence of Christ in the Eucharist or the permanence of marriage. Rejection of traditional teaching and papal authority was dramatically visible in the negative reception of Pope Paul VI's encyclical on birth control, *Humanae Vitae.* Even among some who did not directly contradict Church teaching, a corrosive relativism drained it of content. In many countries, Marxist concepts of class struggle and conflict were preached instead of Christian charity and unity.

Many religious orders suffered both a sharp drop in new members and a mass exodus of existing members, leading in some cases to something approaching collapse. Large numbers of priests left the ministry, and the number of seminarians declined dramatically. In 1970, there were 73,476 priests in North America. During the following twenty-five years, 29,453 new priests were ordained, but 30,393 died and 10,793 left, so that by 1995 there were only 61,743 priests. Europe suffered an even more precipitous decline, from 272,935 priests in 1970 to 217,275 in 1995. In the face of such circumstances, del Portillo, like Escrivá, prayed fervently and did penance, asking our Lord to bring to a swift end the Church's time of trial.

Del Portillo worked to spread the Church's teaching on marriage and sexuality and a sound understanding of the council's teaching, particularly in areas where he had special expertise. In 1969, he published a book entitled *Faithful and Laity in the Church*, one of the first systematic presentations of the council's doctrine on the people of God, which called for an active and responsible participation by all the faithful in the mission of the Church, avoiding both clericalism and passivity. The following year, in response to widespread doubts about priestly identity, he published a book entitled *On Priesthood* which brought together a number of his previously published essays. Building on the teaching of *Presbyterorum Ordinis*, it discusses the identity of priests in terms of their consecration and mission.

In his private correspondence, he encouraged people to be very faithful to the teaching of the Church and not to be scandalized by anything they might see or hear. To a nephew who was a member of a religious order working in the missions he wrote: "Remember what I have told you on other occasions. Be faithful to the traditional doctrine of the Church. . . . Do not omit your prayer, reading, meditation of the Holy Gospel, and little daily mortifications offered to God and to the Most Holy Virgin, our Mother, with fervor and perseverance."

He also encouraged authors who encountered criticism for their loyalty to the Church's teaching. For instance, he wrote to Professor Cornelio Fabro: "You are doing a wonderful service to the Church, our Mother, pointing out clearly the diabolical roots of the evils that afflict us, with so much damage to innumerable souls. May God bless you!" He congratulated the Carmelite Father Philippe de la Trinité on "the clarity of ideas and doctrinal rigor" of his study on Teilhard

de Chardin, which he described as a "truly great service to
the Holy Church and to souls."

In the difficult years following the council, as well is in
the rest of his life, del Portillo showed an openness to new
developments combined with fidelity to the perennial doctrine of the Church. He was careful to distinguish revealed
truth from what is merely the changing patrimony of past
times and different schools of thought. He worked to promote unity, to look for dialogue rather than confrontation,
to stress what unites rather than what divides, and to be sen-
sitive to the fact that most problems, whether political, economic, or social, have a variety of solutions compatible with
Christian faith and morals. For that reason, he strenuously
defended freedom in all its manifestations—religious, cultural, economic, political, educational, artistic—while stressing that authentic freedom goes hand-in-hand with a sense
of responsibility toward the truth that stands in opposition
to relativism.

The Legal Status of Opus Dei

A major focus of del Portillo's life in the decade following
the council was helping Escrivá in his continuing effort to
find an appropriate legal status for Opus Dei.

Opus Dei's assignment to the legal category of secular
institute in 1947 and 1950 had been a painful compromise.
At that time, classification as a secular institute was the
only possible way in which Opus Dei could achieve pontifical approval, but it suggested that the vocation to Opus
Dei involved the "state of perfection," today called consecrated life. This is characteristic of Christians who conse-
crate themselves to God by the three evangelical counsels
of poverty, chastity, and obedience, undertaken by vow or
some equivalent sacred bond and received or recognized by

the hierarchical authority of the Church. In reality, Opus Dei did not involve the state of perfection but rather the effort of each person to achieve Christian perfection in his own state in life, whatever that might be.

To someone without a legal background, this might seem a quibble about words. But thanks to his training in canon law and his experience working on legal issues both for Opus Dei and the Vatican, del Portillo was aware that vital interests were at stake. If Opus Dei was forced to remain for a long time in a legal category which did not fit, there was a danger that the content of the vision Escrivá had received in 1928 might gradually be lost. Despite their involvement in secular affairs, members might eventually come to be regarded as consecrated persons with a special status in the Church, little different from members of religious orders.

That, however, would be fundamentally incompatible with Opus Dei's foundational charism. The Work's basic message involves the call to holiness that all men and women receive as a result of baptism. The call is addressed to every Christian and does not require any consecration other than that of baptism or any status other than that of the ordinary faithful. Treating as special those who decided to take seriously this call to holiness in ordinary life would contradict the message itself.

From the time Opus Dei was first classified as a secular institute, there had been a tension between the Work's reality and what most people, including most Vatican officials, understood secular institutes to be. The legislation establishing the legal framework for secular institutes provided that, as a matter of law, they were normally not to be understood as religious institutes or societies of common life. Most people, however, viewed them, in the words of the authors of a major study of the legal status of Opus Dei, as "an adaptation or rapprochement of the religious state to the world, rather than affirming the Christian potential of the secular or lay condition."

As time passed, many institutions all but indistinguishable from religious orders were approved as secular institutes. Combined with the fact that Vatican officials tended to view secular institutes through the lens of the religious life, that meant that by the early 1960s almost everyone saw secular institutes as a more flexible manifestation of the state of perfection characteristic of religious orders. Thus Escrivá began to say that Opus Dei was not really a secular institute, despite being included in that legal category.

Del Portillo shared Escrivá's desire for a more appropriate legal category for Opus Dei that would respect its fully secular character and that of its members. This became a major focus of his prayer of petition—indeed, probably its principal focus. Along with Escrivá, he prayed intensely to the Blessed Virgin Mary, "*Cor Mariae dulcisimum, inter para tutum* [Most sweet heart of Mary, prepare a safe way]."

He also worked intensely with Escrivá on possible solutions. In 1960, at Escrivá's request he engaged in lengthy conversations with Vatican officials about changing the legal status, but he was told that any changes were still a long way off. Two years later, Escrivá once again requested a change. Besides working intensely on the documents accompanying the petition, del Portillo went with Escrivá on a pilgrimage to the shrine of Our Lady of Pompeii near Naples to ask the Blessed Virgin to grant Opus Dei an appropriate legal framework. Once again, however, the response of the Holy See was negative.

In an audience on October 10, 1964, Pope Paul VI told Escrivá that the documents being prepared by the council might contain a solution. The decree *Presbyterorum ordinis* did, as we have seen, allow for the creation of personal prelatures, a legal structure admirably suited to reflect the reality of Opus Dei. In the mid-1960s, several papal documents fleshed out the necessary framework. Del Portillo played a role in the writing of the most important of these, the motu proprio *Eccelsiae Sanctae*. Now, for the first time in the history of Opus Dei, an appropriate legal category existed in the Church's legislation. But rather than request the immediate transformation of Opus Dei into a personal prelature, Escrivá preferred to continue to wait and pray for the right moment. Don Alvaro joined fervently in his prayer.

Special General Congress of Opus Dei

In 1969, Escrivá called a special general congress of Opus Dei to suggest revisions to its statutes and to prepare the voluminous documentation that would have to be presented to the Holy See. In the months preceding the opening of the congress, Father Alvaro accompanied Escrivá on pilgrimages to numerous shrines of Our Lady in Europe, where they prayed for the Church, for the Pope, and for the work of the upcoming congress. Escrivá explained that they were praying to the Blessed Virgin because she "has been the good Mother who has consoled us, who has smiled at us, who has encouraged us in the difficult moments of our blessed struggle to move forward this army of apostles in the world."

The general congress opened on September 1, 1969. Eighty-seven men and 105 women participated. Del Portillo served as general secretary. At the start, he presented a declaration of unity with the founder and fidelity to his spirit. Many years ago, he pointed out, the Holy See had granted the founder lifetime power to propose changes to Opus Dei's specific law, so that he did not need the approval of anyone in Opus Dei to do this. "If the Father has wanted to call this general congress, we will do all we can to lend our

cooperation joyfully [understanding that] the Father will
freely accept or not accept whatever he thinks appropriate of
what we propose."

The first session lasted two weeks. Having underlined
the need for adequate legal framework for Opus Dei, it suggested the category of personal prelature, as set out in the
documents of the Second Vatican Council and developed
in later pontifical legislation. The general congress agreed
to reconvene in a year's time; in the meantime del Portillo
informed the Holy See that special work sessions would be
organized throughout the world to give all the members an
opportunity to make suggestions for consideration in the
second session.

Storm Clouds

During the first session of the general congress or immediately afterward, Escrivá was shocked to learn indirectly that
a special commission had been established in the Vatican to
study the situation of secular institutes that wished to stop
being treated as such, particularly Opus Dei. The formation
of such a body without consulting or even informing the head
of Opus Dei was alarming, especially since some members
of the commission were known to be hostile to Opus Dei.
A special cause for concern was that Archbishop Giovanni
Benelli, deputy secretary of state for ordinary affairs and a
highly influential figure in the Vatican, was instrumental in
setting up the commission.

A serious misunderstanding had arisen between Benelli
and Opus Dei during 1962 to 1965 when he served as counselor of the Vatican's embassy in Spain. In that capacity, he
worked to distance the Church from the Franco regime. As
part of that effort he asked Escrivá to convince the small
number of Opus Dei members in Franco's government to

As a boy Alvaro's high spirits sometimes got him into trouble, but he displayed great kindness to his younger brothers and sisters in whom he continued to take a real interest throughout his life.

Alvaro was the third of the eight children of Clementina Diez de Solano, the daughter of Mexican landowners, and Ramón del Portillo a Spanish lawyer. Even late in life he still recited frequently prayers he learned from his mother.

Alvaro spent a year and a half as a refugee in the Legation of Honduras during the Spanish Civil War. This photo may have been taken to use on a passport as part of one of his efforts to find a way to leave the legation and escape from the area of Spain where the church was persecuted.

The Spanish School of Civil Engineering was founded in 1802 primarily to serve the needs of the Ministry of Public Works. Its graduates were high ranking civil servants entitled to wear a dress uniform. Alvaro wore his to the Vatican in 1943 when he went to obtain the Holy See's permission for the creation of the Priestly Society of the Holy Cross.

Don Alvaro along with José María Hernández Garnica and José Luis Múzquiz were ordained priests of Opus Dei on June 25, 1944 by the Bishop of Madrid. All three of the first priests of Opus Dei were engineers.

On the day following Don Alvaro's ordination, St. Josemaría asked for his blessing. From that day on Don Alvaro served as his confessor.

Don Alvaro and St. Josemaría often traveled by car to visit the members who were starting Opus Dei in various countries in Europe and to lay the groundwork for its apostolic activities in countries where as yet there were no members of Opus Dei. Here in the Alps in 1949.

In the late 1950s, Don Alvaro accompanied St. Josemaría on several extended visits to England. Along with Fr. Javier Echeverría, the current prelate of Opus Dei, they visited St. Dunstan's church in Canterbury where the head of St. Thomas More is buried.

In the 1950s young women from Europe and North and South America came to Rome to study in the Roman College of Holy Mary and to learn the spirit of Opus Dei directly from the founder. When he met with them, St. Josemaría habitually asked Don Alvaro to accompany him.

Del Portillo celebrated the twenty-fifth anniversary of his ordination in Rome with St. Josemaría, José Luis Múzquiz, and José María Hernández Garnica who came to Rome for the occasion.

During a visit to Guatemala in 1975, St. Josemaría led a round of applause for Don Alvaro on the occasion of the feast of his patron, Blessed Alvaro de Córdoba.

Above: The unexpected death of the founder was a terrible blow to Don Alvaro who had lived with him for 35 years. He choked back his tears and remained calm, however, in order to be able to provide support to the other members of the Work in those difficult days.

Left: At the death of the Founder, Don Alvaro, who had been for decades his shadow, suddenly found himself at the center of attention as the Father of a family composed of sixty thousand men and women on the five continents.

Less than two weeks after his election, St. John Paul II invited Don Alvaro and his two closest aides, Fr. Javier Echeverría and Fr. Joaquín Alonso, to the Vatican, not for a formal audience but for what the Pope described as a family meeting.

Outside of Nullamore Residence in Dublin in August 1980, an eight-year-old boy gave Don Alvaro a rose. He asked that it be placed next to the tabernacle of the residence.

Above Left: On November 30, 1982, Don Alvaro celebrated in Our Lady of Peace, the Church of the Opus Dei Prelature, a solemn Mass of Thanksgiving for the Pope's creation of the Prelature, an intention for which he had prayed and worked for decades.

Above Right: Don Alvaro together with his aides, Fr. Echeverría and Fr. Alonso, frequently visited churches dedicated to the Blessed Virgin. In the photo, leaving the Basilica of St. Mary Major on New Year's day 1983.

Bottom Right: On his trips, Don Alvaro not only spoke to large groups in auditoriums and stadiums but met with individuals from every social strata. Here in 1983.

During a brief visit to the United States in June 1983, Don Alvaro met with many members, friends, and cooperators of Opus Dei in the auditorium of Hunter College in New York. He spoke at length about marriage, urging married couples to love each other with their defects.

Don Alvaro felt special affection for the sick, especially sick children. When he had to go to the clinic of the University of Navarre, for a checkup or for a health problem, he usually visited other patients, particularly seriously ill children.

Neither busyness nor the presence of other people prevented Don Alvaro from giving his full attention to the person he was talking with, even if the conversation was brief.

Each year at Easter thousand of students connected with Opus Dei centers throughout the world converge on Rome for the UNIV international student congress. Among the highlights of the trip are an audience with the Holy Father and a get together with the Prelate of Opus Dei. Some lucky students met with the Prelate personally. Here is a group from Japan.

At the beginning of a get together in Nairobi, Kenya in April 1989, Don Alvaro received a spear and a shield as part of his induction as an elder.

Right: Wherever he went, Don Alvaro made time to meet with families. Here in Nairobi, Kenya in 1989.

Although Opus Dei's apostolic activities in the Ivory Coast had begun less than ten years earlier, when Don Alvaro visited the country in 1989 so many people wanted to see and hear him that they had to organize a get together in one of the largest auditoriums of Abidjan.

© L'Osservatore Romano

Don Alvaro was ordained Bishop by St. John Paul II in St. Peter's Basilica on the feast of the Epiphany in January 1991. He described his ordination as "a new outpouring of the Holy Spirit on the head of the Work and, because of the communion of the saints, in some way on all of Opus Dei. It will move the Work forward all over the world. It will be a great gift of God."

On March 22, 1994, at the end of his pilgrimage to the Holy Land, Don Alvaro celebrated Mass in the Church of the Cenacle where Jesus celebrated the Last Supper. It would prove to be his last mass, since he died early in the morning of March 23rd.

In an unusual show of esteem and affection, St. John Paul II left the Vatican to come to Don Alvaro's wake in the Church of the Opus Dei Prelature, Our Lady of Peace.

resign their positions. Escrivá refused, on the grounds that members of Opus Dei enjoy complete political freedom and the Work could not and should not try to influence their political decisions. If the Spanish hierarchy thought they should officially call on all Catholics to refuse to cooperate with the government, members of Opus Dei, like other Catholics, would of course be obliged to do that. But Opus Dei, he explained, could not tell its members what to think or do in politics.

Benelli did not take kindly to this. Relations between the two men became cold, possibly because Benelli failed to understand that Escrivá was not motivated by a desire to support the Franco regime but by the need to defend a basic characteristic of the spirit of Opus Dei, the political freedom of its members.

Whatever the cause, Bishop Benelli's hostility, or at least coldness, was a cause of serious concern in the late 1960s, since he had become one of the most influential figures in the Vatican, described by *Time* magazine in 1967 as Pope Paul's "powerful number two."

The future cardinal would eventually come to have great confidence in del Portillo, whose advice and help he frequently sought after becoming Archbishop of Florence. He also wrote to the Pope suggesting that Escrivá's cause of canonization be begun. Del Portillo, for his part, treated him from the beginning not only with respect but with sincere affection, which may explain his eventual change of attitude. In the 1960s, however, he was anything but well disposed toward Opus Dei.

With the help of del Portillo and others, Escrivá wrote directly to the Holy Father on September 16, 1969. Attached to the letter was a summary of what had transpired during the first part of the special general congress and a lengthy note explaining why he requested that no decisions be made about the legal status of Opus Dei while the special general congress was still in session.

A few days later, the secretary of state called to say that, although the commission did exist, its only purpose was to study the situation of secular institutes made up of priests. He added that some expressions in the letter had upset the Pope. Escrivá immediately wrote another letter, explaining the origin and significance of his previous letter and again expressing his filial loyalty to the Pope. "I ask Your Holiness to pardon with all your heart whatever displeasure I may have caused you, certainly against my will. With the greatest confidence I place in your hands my desires to clarify this question, fully aware that the paternal concern of the Supreme Pastor will find the best way to receive them, understand them, and fully satisfy them." Escrivá also went twice to see Benelli in an attempt to clear things up, but his reception was cold and even mistrustful. Shortly thereafter, the secretary of state wrote a letter requesting the names of the members of Opus Dei working in the curia. The request was an unusual one that seemed to suggest mistrust. Nonetheless, Escrivá immediately responded with the requested information. Once again, del Portillo as Escrivá's closest collaborator and confidant shared his distress.

We Fly to Your Patronage

In the spring of 1970, del Portillo accompanied Escrivá on several pilgrimages, traveling to Fatima and to Torrreciudad in northern Spain where members of Opus Dei, with the help of many others, were building a large shrine to the Mother of God. Shortly after their return, del Portillo visited Cardinal Dell'Acqua, the Pope's vicar for the diocese of Rome, to explain to him why Opus Dei wished to become into a personal prelature.

On May 1, 1970, Escrivá announced that he had decided to make a pilgrimage to our Lady of Guadalupe in Mexico, accompanied by Don Alvaro. There they made a novena to Our Lady, spending hours each day praying to her for the Church, the Pope, and for Opus Dei. Del Portillo and Escrivá returned from Mexico full of confidence that our Lady of Guadalupe, to whom they had prayed with such fervor, would resolve sooner or later the question of Opus Dei's legal status.

Second Session

The second session of the general congress studied more than 50,000 notes and suggestions contributed by members all over the world. The delegates unanimously approved a resolution requesting that the founder "renew, at the time and in the way that he thinks opportune, his humble and confident request that the Holy See resolve definitively the institutional problem of Opus Dei." With that, the second session closed.

Although the main sessions were over, the congress had not officially concluded, and a small technical commission of canon lawyers was established to study, together with del Portillo and the founder, Opus Dei's particular law in the light of the conclusions of the congress. The process of elaborating a new statute for Opus Dei was long and laborious, but a new statute was approved by the founder on October 1, 1974. At that point, it became a question of waiting for the opportune moment to ask the Holy See to designate Opus a personal prelature. This would change its legal classification and transfer authority over it from the Congregation for Religious and Secular Institutes to the Congregation for Bishops, without modifying its substance, its spirit, or its role in the life of the Church. No further steps had been taken when Escrivá died unexpectedly on June 26, 1975. It would be up to del Portillo to complete the process.

Accompanying Escrivá on His Catechetical Trips

During his stay in Mexico in 1970, Escrivá met with a number of large groups of members of Opus Dei, cooperators, and other people in contact with the Work's apostolate, speaking with them very informally about the faith and, above all, answering their questions. These get-togethers in Mexico, which del Portillo attended faithfully, did much to set the pattern for much larger sessions in other countries during the final three years of the founder's life.

Although Escrivá sometimes referred to his get-togethers with large numbers of people as catechetical, that seems to suggest something much more formal and structured than the real-life encounters. In most cases, Escrivá talked for no more than ten minutes before opening the floor to questions, which came flooding in. People asked about everything: how to love the Blessed Virgin more, how to do apostolate with fellow students, how to make better use of time, how to deal with difficult situations at home or at work, and a host of other topics.

Escrivá created around him such a warm and intimate environment that the questioners showed no hesitation about posing before hundreds and even thousands of people questions that obviously reflected personal concerns. Escrivá, for his part, made a point of responding directly to the questioner, almost as if they were alone. When the groups were large and the questioners had microphones, he asked that someone stand next to each one with a small red light on a pole so that he could more easily locate the person and address him or her directly. His answers were usually short and always positive and encouraging.

Escrivá first long catechetical trip took him to Spain and Portugal in fall 1972. In spring 1974, a second lengthy trip took him to Brazil, Argentina, Chile, Peru, Ecuador, and Venezuela. On that trip he planned to go on to Guatemala, but health problems forced him to cut short the trip. He returned to Venezuela and Guatemala in February 1975. Shortly after reaching Guatemala, however, health problems once again intervened, and he returned to Rome.

Del Portillo accompanied Escrivá on these trips and attended virtually all the get-togethers. During one in Barcelona, a woman told Escrivá that a friend of hers who had attended a previous get-together was impressed by the obvious affection with which del Portillo listened to things he must have heard dozens or hundreds of times before. Her friend, she said, remarked upon how much affection people in Opus Dei had for each other. Escrivá responded: "She's right. We love each other! And that's the greatest compliment people can pay us, because the pagans affirmed about the first faithful, 'Look how they love one another.'"

Bishop Echevarría, who also accompanied Escrivá on these trips, commented: "I always saw Don Alvaro eclipsed, in the background but in a spot where he could see, hear, and take care of our Father. He looked at him . . . with a desire to learn from him. . . . I always saw him attentive to our founder, backing him up in everything, to help him carry out Opus Dei." Especially during the last two trips, del Portillo's service to the founder expressed itself in care for his health—urging him to rest and take the time required to recover from the illnesses he suffered.

Besides supporting Escrivá, del Portillo also contributed greatly to fostering family spirit among the members of Opus Dei he encountered during these trips. Said one: "Alvaro has shown his affection for each one of us in small ways, with pleasant comments and opportune questions. He

was careful not to draw attention to himself, but he radiated
warmth and affection in a quiet way." The person who kept
the diary of the Opus Dei center where they stayed in Mexico City wrote: "Don Alvaro has also impressed all of us.
He is always at the Father's side, with a fidelity and refinement in dealing with him that is the best example we could
hope for. On more than one occasion when Don Alvaro was
not present, the Father has praised him. But even if he had
not done so, we could not fail to notice the support and the
affection he gives the Father. . . . He has given us a model
of how to deal with the Father."

Del Portillo succeeded in convincing the founder to allow
the large-scale get-togethers to be filmed. At first, Escrivá
resisted, but Don Alvaro won him over by pointing out that
if the get-togethers weren't filmed, later generations would
think that his sons who were with him either were stupid or
did not love him. "Stupid we may be," said del Portillo, "but
not that stupid. And certainly we do love you."

CHAPTER 14

SUCCEEDING THE FOUNDER

As the 1970s wore on, the cardiac insufficiency from which Escrivá suffered gradually grew worse. He also had vision problems, a consequence of diabetes. Yet in 1975 neither del Portillo nor the other people closest to him expected him to die soon.

On June 25, the founder joined the members of the general council in celebrating the anniversary of the ordination of del Portillo and the other two who were the first priests of Opus Dei. In the get-together after the midday meal, they were served a glass of a Hungarian liqueur sent by a professor who had received it as a gift from a friend. As was his custom, Escrivá did not try it and for some reason asked del Portillo not to have any. The Father exhibited his usual lighthearted good humor, commenting on the curiosity on people's faces as they waited to taste the unfamiliar liqueur.

The next morning, after Mass and a light breakfast, del Portillo and Don Javier Echevarría accompanied Escrivá to Opus Dei's international center of formation for women in Castel Gandolfo. After a few minutes of informal conversation that included his urging the women to have a priestly soul, the founder began to feel ill and had to cut short the get-together. After resting briefly in the priest's office, he announced that he was ready to return to Rome. Del Portillo tried to convince him to rest a bit longer, but he insisted he was well enough to leave.

Returning to Villa Tevere a few minutes before noon, Escrivá had such difficulty getting up the stairs that del Portillo feared he might die on the spot. Nevertheless, the founder stopped briefly to greet our Lord in the Blessed Sacrament with a slow, devout genuflection and an act of love. Seconds after entering del Portillo's office, where he usually worked, Escrivá called out to his secretary, Javier Echevarría, "Javi! Javi, I don't feel well!" and fell to the floor. A doctor, who happened to be close by, immediately tried to bring him around with oxygen, injections, and heart massage. Del Portillo gave him absolution and administered the anointing of the sick. During the next hour and a half, they tried to save the founder's life while del Portillo several times repeated absolution. He also called the director of the women's branch and asked her to have the members who were in the central headquarters go to the oratory and pray for at least ten minutes with great intensity for a very urgent intention. At 1:30, he finally yielded to the evidence that the founder was dead.

Del Portillo's first thought as he held the Father's dead body in his arms was, "Now we have really been left orphans." But he immediately corrected that: "We have not been left orphans. We are not orphans. God, who is our Father, is in heaven. In addition, we have there with Him our founder . . ."

The members of the general counsel were sobbing, but Don Alvaro, as the oldest brother of the family, could not give into grief. He arranged for news of the founder's death to be communicated to the members of Opus Dei throughout the world, as well as to the Holy See and to the press, and started making arrangements for the funeral and for the Masses that would be said continuously in the oratory where the founder would be waked.

Another decision was what inscription to put on the founder's tomb. Back in 1957, Escrivá had said his preference was *"Iosephmaria Escrivá De Balaguer y Albas. Peccator. Orate Pro Eo"* (Josemaría Escrivá de Balaguer y Albas. A Sinner. Pray for him). If they liked, he added, they might add *"Genuit Filios Et Filias* [He Fathered Sons and Daughters]," but when the time came, they could, he said, do whatever they thought best. Don Alvaro knew that for years the founder had signed himself "Josemaría, the sinner," but in conscience he felt they could not put this on the founder's tomb. Rather, he chose the simple phrase *"El Padre"* (The Father).

Despite all he had to attend to and the sorrow in his heart that made it difficult to think clearly, del Portillo composed within three days of Escriva's death a letter of some six thousand words to all members of the Work recounting the founder's death and funeral. Stressing the importance of humility, he urged them to "ask our Lord, through the intercession of the Father, to grant to each of us the grace of a holy hunger to disappear, to be the last, to obey with greater finesse than ever." Theirs, he reminded them, should be lives of solid piety marked by a desire to "convert each one [of the norms of their plan of life] into a more intimate encounter with God."

Although he very likely felt Escrivá's death more deeply than anyone else, he concentrated on helping the others, as Bishop Echevarría wrote later, by "supporting everyone with fortitude and an extraordinary peace." Of his letter to the members, a Portuguese biographer of del Portillo says, "He, the man of a smile and of silence, poured into the letter everything that he carried in his heart. He did not hesitate to interpret the thought of the founder, now absent, and to speak in his name."

Election as President General

As secretary general, del Portillo automatically assumed leadership of Opus Dei, pending an election to choose a successor to the founder. Escrivá had wanted no turmoil after he died. Many ecclesiastical institutions had suffered a virtual trauma in these circumstances, but there was to be nothing of that sort in the Work. Having interiorized that principle and wanting to avoid upsetting plans already made in many regions for formational activities during the summer, del Portillo set September 14 as the date for the opening of the electoral congress.

For decades it had been clear that del Portillo was the person Escrivá had identified and meticulously trained as his successor. Just two days before his death, he pointed to del Portillo and said to Msgr. Alonso, "My son, if you're not foolish, when I die you will follow that brother of yours." Del Portillo nevertheless did not take his election as a foregone conclusion.

In a homily preached at a Mass of the Holy Spirit which he celebrated to open the electoral congress, he again stressed the importance of humility: "God's grace penetrates like a ray of light in a humble soul where it shimmers. Pride, on the other hand, cuts the ray of light and leaves the soul in darkness." After again calling for fidelity to the spirit of the founder, he concluded: "We should prefer to die a thousand times rather than be unfaithful!"

On one occasion, a member of the Work who was chatting with him while waiting for dinner to be served referred to an event as having occurred "in the times of our Father." Del Portillo immediately corrected him with a smile, "In the Work," he said, "we are always in the times of our Father."

To no one's surprise, the congress unanimously chose del Portillo as Escrivá's successor on September 15, 1975. He told the electors that they had chosen him "because you knew that

I had spent more time than anyone else at our Father's side, and you were looking for continuity. You have not voted for Alvaro del Portillo but rather have elected our Father." When immediately after the election he went to pray at Escrivá's tomb, members of the Work who were there began to stand as a sign of respect. "Don't stand," Don Alvaro told them using a Spanish saying translated as, "In the presence of the captain, the sailor gives no orders, and the captain is there." He then knelt down, kissed the tombstone, and said, "Ask him that he be the one to direct the Work from heaven, and that we who succeed him may be only instruments of his and nothing more. If the Father, being a saint, asked us to pray for him, you can imagine how much prayer I need who am not at all a saint. You have an even greater obligation . . . to pray for me. I really need everyone's prayers."

The request for prayer became a leitmotif in Don Alvaro's life; over and over again, he begged the members of Opus Dei as well as others to pray for him. At the start of his first audience with Pope Paul VI as head of Opus Dei, for instance, he asked the Pope to pray for him. "I am the successor of a saint, and that is nothing easy," he explained. To which Pope Paul replied, "But now the saint is in heaven, and he'll take care of things."

The Successor's Tasks

Every successor of Escrivá will face the challenge of guiding Opus Dei, promoting the zeal and good spirit of its members, deciding on priorities in its apostolates, and above all being Father of this small portion of the Church, fostering a spirit of fraternity and filiation that will maintain the family spirit with which Opus Dei was born. Del Portillo faced all these challenges, but in addition he had to find a way of being the head of Opus Dei without being its founder. A number of special tasks faced him. Most important, the founder had specifically charged him with bringing to completion the search for an adequate place for Opus Dei in the Church's legal structure. Thanks to the Second Vatican Council and the legislation subsequently enacted under Pope Paul VI, a category perfectly suited to Opus Dei, that of personal prelature, now existed. But the challenge for del Portillo, no small one, was to persuade the Holy See to apply that legislation to Opus Dei.

Escrivá had also left him a smaller but still very important charge to annotate the entries the founder had made off and on over a number of years in series of notebooks where he recorded important events in his own spiritual life and the life of Opus Dei (known in Spanish as his *Apuntes íntimos*). He had hoped to find time to clarify his often somewhat cryptic entries by explaining their context, the events that gave rise to them, the people involved, etc. Lacking such notes, many entries would be difficult for future readers to understand. But he had not managed to do that, and he left a written request that Don Alvaro, who knew better than anyone else what was involved, do the job.

A related task was to prepare for publication a number of books Escrivá had written but had been unable to put in final form. Most manuscripts needed little more than final editing, but that would take considerable time. Others could certainly help, but del Portillo was uniquely qualified to oversee the process.

Finally, Don Alvaro had to take at least the initial steps to prepare for the eventual canonization of the founder. Having lived so close to Escrivá for so many years, he was intimately convinced of his sanctity. Because the founder had lived the spirit of Opus Dei with extraordinary fidelity, his canonization would also be a new formal expression of the Church's approval of that spirit as a way of seeking sanctity in the midst of the world.

Shortly after his election, del Portillo began to suffer serious health problems. The Italian specialist he consulted diagnosed them as symptoms of advanced liver cancer that would soon prove fatal. But when three doctors from the University of Navarre Clinic who had taken care of him for years were asked for a second opinion, they concluded that he did not have liver cancer but was suffering a reaction to a pain reliever he was taking for the strong headaches he had long suffered. Once he stopped taking that medicine, he returned to normal.

The first doctor's diagnosis had not been explicitly shared with del Portillo, but he knew the physician was alarmed. While accepting the will of God, he said later, he had been thinking about what he should do so that his death so soon after the founder's death would not cause problems in Opus Dei.

CHAPTER 15

A MAN OF PRAYER
AND A FATHER

Many factors combine to shape del Portillo's activities during the two decades in which he led Opus Dei, but two deserve special attention: his life of prayer and his commitment to being "the Father" for the members.

A Man of Prayer

During a pilgrimage to the Shrine of Our Lady of Czestochowa in Poland in 1979, del Portillo said, "We have come to pray, and to pray, and then to pray some more." That was his personal formula not only during that pilgrimage but during the years in which he headed Opus Dei, and indeed during his entire life.

By the time he became head of the Work, he had struggled for forty years to become a man of prayer—in Escrivá's phrase, "a contemplative soul in the midst of the world." To the end of his life, Don Alvaro practiced each day the plan of life he had learned at the beginning of his vocation to Opus Dei, seeking to carry it out with ever greater love and care in the conviction that his new obligations made it all the more necessary.

The Eucharist

The Mass was the center and root of his interior life. No matter how pressing the demands on del Portillo's time, he took pains to celebrate Mass each day in a recollected manner. His highest priority when making travel plans was that there be adequate time for Mass. The priest who normally served his Mass described him as celebrating it "with great recollection, slowly, absorbed in the mystery."

His love of Jesus in the Eucharist showed itself in other ways, such as frequent visits to the Blessed Sacrament. When traveling by car, he prayed to Jesus in the tabernacles of churches along the way and pointed them out to his companions so they could do the same. Even late in life, del Portillo genuflected slowly and carefully, without making concessions to the increasing difficulty arising from age and lumbar problems. When he had to preside at concelebrated Masses and on other occasions calling for singing, he worked hard to master the chants, though lacking a good ear and voice. The day before a ceremony, he would carefully study the parts he had to sing and in the evening listen to a tape. When the moment arrived, he sang his best, without worrying about it if he sang off key or missed the melody.

Habitually, he prayed aloud together with his two aides the psalms and readings that make up the breviary. They normally prayed the first part in the morning and the rest in the late afternoon. The breviary helped him to be deeply united to the Church's liturgy and provided material for his personal prayer and his preaching.

Mental Prayer

The half hour before Mass del Portillo spent before the Blessed Sacrament, meditating together with the members of Opus Dei's general council. In the afternoon he gave another half hour to mental prayer. For long periods of his life he arrived in the oratory half an hour before the scheduled start of the morning meditation to have more time for mental prayer.

Del Portillo described mental prayer as "the conversation of people in love: a conversation in which there is no place for boredom or distraction; a heart-to-heart talk to which we look forward impatiently, to which we go with a hunger to get to know Jesus better and really relate to him; a conversation conducted with the delicacy of a soul in love and which ends with a renewed desire to live and work only for the Lord." People would come and go while he was praying in the crypt where St. Josemaría is buried, but he did not notice them. Talking silently with Jesus absorbed him completely.

These periods of mental prayer were for del Portillo not a burdensome obligation to be fitted somehow into the day but appointments with Our Lord and His Mother to which he looked forward and around which other things were arranged. This did not mean a rigid or slavish insistence on making his meditation every day at the same time; but he did show a strong preference for the usual time, and if for some important reason a change was necessary, he preferred to pray earlier in the day rather than later. In any case, he looked for a time and a place where he could dedicate all his energies to talking with God without interruptions or distractions.

The Blessed Mother and St. Joseph

Del Portillo's devotion to the Blessed Virgin manifested itself in many ways. Perhaps the most striking was his designation of three consecutive Marian years in Opus Dei. The first, in 1978, marked the fiftieth anniversary of the Work's founding. At its conclusion, he extended it for another year to mark the fiftieth anniversary of the beginning of Opus Dei's work with women. So pleased was he with the spiritual fruits of these two Marian years that he declared a third one, which concluded on December 31, 1980.

During the Marian years, he entrusted to the Blessed Virgin in a special way the project of finding an appropriate legal status for Opus Dei in the Church, the cause of canonization of the founder, and the expansion of Opus Dei's apostolic activities to new countries. The years were not isolated events in his life, and he hoped they would not be in the lives of his sons and daughters in Opus Dei. "These Marian years," he wrote, "have left in our souls the profound conviction that all of our time on earth—and afterwards, with the grace of God, in the marvelous eternity of heaven—has become a Marian time."

He frequently invoked the Blessed Mother with traditional prayers like the Memorare, the Salve Regina, and above all the Rosary. He prayed the Angelus and all fifteen decades of the Rosary daily, and on long car trips, he often prayed many more decades. When he said the Rosary aloud during the monthly day of recollection he made with the members of the general council, he stood rather than sat to keep from being overcome by drowsiness. In the years before Opus Dei became a personal prelature, whenever he was in Rome, he made a weekly visit to at least one church dedicated to Our Lady, saying one part of the Rosary on the way there, one part at the church, and one part on the way home.

In thanksgiving for John Paul II's decision to make Opus Dei a personal prelature, he went on a pilgrimage to the shrine of Our Lady of Guadalupe in Mexico City and there made a novena to the Blessed Virgin, spending hours each day praying before her image. At the end of the novena, he commented: "Her face shows an utter simplicity. Her expression is one of sweetness, of humility, of purity, of honesty. It's a look of compassion, of love, and, at the same time, of suffering. I think that she suffered when she saw that no one was paying any attention to poor Juan Diego, and that she is looking at him with compassion and affection. I thought of your sins and mine, and I realized that she is looking at us, too, with that great affection—because she is our mother—but also, at times, with sorrow. . . . Let us not cause our Mother in heaven any sorrow."

Love for the Blessed Virgin was for him closely related to the Eucharist, to the point that he sometimes referred to the Mass as "the great Marian devotion." He was aware of her presence in the Mass, which echoed her presence on Calvary. In the Blessed Sacrament Chapel which he had built in Opus Dei's prelatic church, he had the inside of the tabernacle decorated with medals of Our Lady. For that purpose, he asked his children in each country to send a medal with a representation of her that was especially popular there.

Love for the Blessed Virgin was not simply one more devotion; it was a dimension of his life. He imitated her faith, her humility, her spirit of service, and her habit of keeping in her heart everything Jesus did and said. Even as he entered old age, his love of Our Lady continued to develop. In 1983, for instance, he discovered a new meaning in the fact that Mary is *our* mother: She was at the same time his mother and Jesus' mother. "Now it's as if two brothers are talking about their mother," he said.

He also had great devotion to St. Joseph. During one of Escrivá's trips to Latin America, the founder advised a recently widowed woman to put a statute of St. Joseph in her home and to ask him to act as head of her family. Del Portillo apparently was following that advice when, shortly after his election, he asked that a statue of St. Joseph be placed in the living room where he habitually joined the members of the General Council for a half hour of informal conversation in the evening.

He cultivated spiritual childhood. On one occasion, he said, "Following in the footsteps of our Father, I want . . . to be always little—more so every day—so that I can find for myself a good place in the arms of Mary, in the arms of Joseph, very close to our Jesus." Meeting with an enthusiastic group of young people in Nigeria, he said, "I am also young because I am in love with God, and love is always young. It never grows old. I am younger than you are, although I am seventy-five years old."

Spirit of Sacrifice

He responded generously to Christ's invitation to "take up his cross each day." Escrivá's aspiration, *"In laetitia, nulla dies sine cruce"* (In joy, no day without the cross) was a reality in his life. It was expresssed in traditional Christian practices of asceticism like the use of the cilice and the disciplines, but above all in the intensity of his work, the loving fulfillment of his other duties, his focus on the needs and concerns of others and of the Church, and the cheerfulness and good humor with which he bore illness.

One of the doctors who took care of him described him as "striking in his abandonment in the hands of God in everything that referred to his health. He wanted to be well in order to be able to work effectively, but at the same time he accepted with optimism and joy the limitations and pains of ill health, seeing in them caresses from his Father God." In the final years of his life, he often slept poorly, yet he continued to get up on time and put in a full day's work, often reaching the end of the day exhausted—but with a cheerful smile.

In June 1993, on the forty-ninth anniversary of his priestly ordination and just nine months before his death, he spoke briefly about his approaching golden anniversary with characteristic detachment from the question of health and even from life itself: "There is still a year to go, in which many things can happen. I ask our Lord to help me be faithful minute by minute, day by day. In that way I prepare for my priestly jubilee, if it arrives. . . . And if not, I will celebrate it in Paradise. Wherever God wants. It's more comfortable to go, too comfortable. I want whatever the Lord wants."

This was not an isolated sentiment. Every night before going to sleep, he told Our Lord he was ready to die "when you want, where you want, and as you want." When, as sometimes happened, this prayer made him feel a bit afraid, he would repeat it, adding: "with the condition that it be in your hands." Beginning in 1975 or thereabouts, he added, "right now, if you want, but with an act of perfect contrition and if possible with the last sacraments."

He practiced small voluntary mortifications like sitting for a time without leaning against the back of the chair or waiting before drinking a glass of water on hot days. He tried to follow Escrivá's advice to put aside his own tastes and interests in order to make life more pleasant for others. Since his youth, he had had a great love for the sea. But one summer day, at an informal get-together near the seashore, he chose a chair facing away from the ocean in order to leave the chairs with a view for others. The ocean aside, he had little interest in excursions in the countryside, but when a member of Opus Dei was visiting who especially enjoyed seeing places of natural beauty, del Portillo took advantage of a holiday to invite him to "accompany him" on a visit to a scenic area outside Rome, though he would have preferred staying home and reading a book.

Living in God's Presence

Mental prayer, the Mass, the breviary and the Rosary, as well as other practices of piety like spiritual reading and examination of conscience, took up a significant portion of his day, but he did not limit himself to praying only at times specially set aside for prayer. These, rather, were necessary means for turning his entire day into a conversation with God. Even in the final years of his life, he continued to work at cultivating an awareness of God's presence during the day and turning frequently to our Lord or his Blessed Mother—to ask help, to give thanks, to offer praise, to ask forgiveness. On his birthday and on important anniversaries, for instance, he habitually prayed a brief aspiration: "Thank you. Pardon me. Help me more."

To remind himself of God's presence while working, he kept on his desk a number of holy cards with images of Our Lady which he changed daily. Following a suggestion of Escrivá's, he dedicated each day of the week to a particular devotion: Sunday, the Holy Trinity; Monday, the Souls in Purgatory; Tuesday, the Guardian Angels; Wednesday, St. Joseph; Thursday, the Eucharist; Friday, the Holy Cross; and Saturday, Our Lady.

In time he acquired an habitual, loving awareness of God's presence. As his first biographer wrote, he was "attentive to those around him, but at the same time immersed in God and in the things of God. He truly was, to borrow the words of the founder of Opus Dei, 'in heaven and on earth.' He lived a contemplative life in the midst of the activities of the world."

Awareness of God's presence was, as the Australian Cardinal Edward Cassidy noted, the source of his characteristic peace and calm. The head of Opus Dei in Spain recalls that when he went to Rome, he often met with del Portillo toward the end of the evening, and sometimes they discussed difficult and annoying problems. But when they called an end to the conversation and took part in an informal get-together with other members of the General Council, del Portillo entered at once into the lighthearted talk with a smile as if he hadn't a care in the world.

His deep interior life of prayer and sacrifice was reflected in many other everyday ways. His ordinary conversation was punctuated with phrases like "Thanks be to God," "How good God is!" and "God bless you!" These weren't trite expressions in his mouth but authentic, spontaneous prayers. His conversation and preaching were optimistic and cheerful. He communicated hope that, with God's help, everything can change, that sanctity is not a utopia, that although human affairs are always marked by trials, Christ triumphs precisely through the cross. On one occasion, he commented, "It is very good for us to suffer difficulties and misunderstandings, because . . . it makes us keep rectifying our intentions."

Because of his own interior life of prayer and sacrifice, he strove to help his listeners to discover Christ, to enjoy the truth of being God's children, to take advantage of Mary's protection, to become more prayerful, and to understand that their efforts to come closer to God are not based primarily on their own will but on the grace that comes from the sacraments.

A Father to His Sons and Daughters

The second factor underlying del Portillo's direction of Opus Dei was being a father to the members of the Work. Opus Dei is hardly alone in describing itself as a family, but a family spirit plays an unusually important role in its life. The sense of being children of God is the foundation of its spirit;

and a sense of being sons and daughters of the head of Opus Dei, called by the members "the Father," is an important part of their lives and promotes a vigorous sense of fraternity. Being the Father to Opus Dei as a whole and to its individual members is in some ways the most important task of the head of Opus Dei and colors all the rest.

Escrivá had been the founder as well as the Father. Del Portillo handled the challenge of being the Father but not the founder with what Cardinal Herranz called "dynamic fidelity." He saw preserving and transmitting the spirit God had given to Escrivá as his principal task, but he understood that he could not simply repeat in rote fashion things Escrivá had said. Dynamic fidelity meant responding to new situations and challenges as the founder would have done and helping the members of Opus Dei all over the world do the same in their diverse circumstances.

Escrivá was an extraordinarily warm human being. He had a deep interior life and lived in the presence of God to a remarkable degree, but he was also an ebullient extrovert with a great capacity to love. He won the adherence and affection of the men and women of Opus Dei not only through his spiritual message but also through his warmth and affection. Del Portillo also had a big, caring heart, but unlike Escrivá he was quiet and reserved, and he had to find ways of expressing his fatherhood compatible with that temperament. His affection and concern manifested themselves in all sorts of ways, big and small: in generous prayer and penance, in tiny gestures, and in the effort to transmit the spirit of the Work. He was able to say, "I live only to think about our Father, about how to be more faithful to him, and about you, how to help you be saints."

He cheerfully went out of his way to make life pleasant for those around him. While spending several weeks in an old country house, he learned that drawing water first thing in the morning for the hot bath his doctor had prescribed left someone else without hot water for shaving. He immediately changed his bath time so the other person would have hot water.

Sending personal birthday or anniversary greetings to the more than 75,000 members of the Work was obviously out of the question, but he made a point of remembering the birthdays of his closest collaborators and writing to them if they were away from Rome. Typically, sanctity was his theme, as when he wrote one member on his birthday in 1985, "May our Lord, with your persevering correspondence to grace, make you very holy."

Concern for the Sick

He was especially attentive to those who were suffering. "There is no suffering of yours, children of my soul, that is not mine," he said. Once a member of the Work returning from his mother's funeral arrived in the middle of the afternoon when del Portillo was engrossed in work; but instead of merely extending condolences, del Portillo asked him to describe in detail his mother's last days in the hope that he might find consolation in this way.

During the final stage of the process of obtaining approval of Opus Dei as a prelature, Don Alvaro was under great pressure, but he didn't forget that the father of a visiting member of the Work was ill or fail to ask how he was doing. About the same time, the mother of a member of the General Council underwent surgery for a brain tumor. Del Portillo frequently asked how her recovery was going and added that he was praying for her.

He visited sick members whenever he could. For example, on a trip from Madrid to Pamplona, he stopped at Saragossa to visit a young woman who'd been badly burned in a car accident. Years later, she wrote in a newspaper article: "There are times when it is very hard to keep a positive outlook on life, and one of those is when your whole life has changed because of an accident . . . The Father told me that even though it is hard to understand, pain is actually a caress from God. He literally said that. And he said it with such conviction that it raised me to his level, the level of faith."

He visited a young priest left completely paralyzed after an accident. The young man reported being impressed by "his extraordinary tenderness, something out of the ordinary. . . . He made me consider how effective my life could and should be despite the lack of physical mobility. . . . I think what most stunned me was a deep impression of being intensely loved by the Father."

In 1988 in Washington, D.C., he visited one of the oldest members of the Work, who had lost a leg in an accident years earlier and was very debilitated by age. Along with encouraging him to place his confidence in God, he asked the man to sing a popular song that del Portillo knew he had liked when he was young.

When he couldn't visit, he wrote. To one of the first members of Opus Dei in Japan, who was dying, he sent a lengthy, handwritten letter that read in part: "I entrust you constantly to our Lord through the intercession of our Father, so that, if it is his will he grant you health. Ask him for it with much faith, also through our Father's intercession. Tell our Father that I have told you so. Don't get tired of asking. . . . That is how you have to be: very much in God, with great desires of working for him and for his Work. At the same time be filled with joy thinking about the moment in which Our Mother will take your soul to heaven, where you will see the Lord, and where she will look at you and smile at you as your mother. Ask to be cured, but accept with joy whatever God wants. Bearing your illness in this way, you are, I want you to remember, a treasure for the Work. Would you like to apply part of that treasure for me? I envy you. Your Father Alvaro recalls you, prays for you, embraces you, and blesses you with all affection. Let me ask you to tell your mother and your brother that I am very united to them."

Besides praying for the sick and visiting them, he tried to see to it that they were well cared for. In the case of celibate members who lived in Opus Dei centers, he encouraged the other members to try to care for them at home, difficult as that might be and even though it might seem they would get better care in a nursing home.

When an early member of Opus Dei in Ireland was diagnosed with leukemia, the specialists concluded that his death was imminent. But del Portillo refused to give up. He suggested seeking a second opinion at the clinic of the University of Navarre, and there the doctors were able to extend the man's life by another three-and-a-half years.

A numerary member of the Work living in Rome was well on her way to recovery from a heart attack when del Portillo heard that a heat wave was coming. The center where she lived was not air-conditioned, so he suggested she go for a while to a place with a cooler climate.

Support in Difficulties

Crises and special problems also elicited del Portillo's affection and support. Shortly after Opus Dei was approved as a personal prelature, a German media company launched a campaign involving nine television programs and thirteen radio programs that described the Work as a religious sect and a dangerous secret society. Opus Dei, it said, was even engaging in arms trafficking. At the same time, parents of young people involved in Opus Dei activities received anonymous pamphlets warning them of the supposed dangers to which their children were exposed. Del Portillo supported his German sons and daughters closely during this difficult time, not only writing to them but traveling frequently to Germany and urging them to redouble their apostolic efforts and not be intimidated.

Escrivá's typical response in the face of these attacks had been to be silent, to pray, to smile, and continue working, but these new calumnies were so vicious and so widely disseminated that del Portillo decided to follow the advice of Cardinal Höffner, the chairman of the Conference of German Bishops, and take legal action. On two separate occasions, German courts ruled in favor of Opus Dei and said the attacks violated fundamental human rights. The stations were required to broadcast formal retractions. For some time, nevertheless, the atmosphere in Germany remained poisoned, and del Portillo maintained particularly close contact with the members of the Work there.

The German attacks spilled over into Austria, fueled by a book illustrated with photos of Ku Klux Klan ceremonies and engravings of the Inquisition and medieval tortures. A priest of the Work, the chaplain in a high school in Vienna, was attacked for supposedly obliging young students to take vows of chastity and giving them holy water to drink to see if they were possessed. Austrian critics of St. John Paul II intensified their attacks on Opus Dei when it became known that he intended to name a priest of Opus Dei as bishop of an Austrian diocese. Del Portillo was especially close to his sons and daughters in Austria during these trying times, making fifteen trips to visit them and writing them frequently. Among other things, he told them not to speak about the calumnies even among themselves, lest they fail in charity or become discouraged in the apostolate.

He gave particular attention to countries where Opus Dei was just getting started and the few members faced particular difficulties. In 1989, visiting the only center of Opus Dei in Cameroon, he told the members: "My children, you are just beginning. You are the seed sown by the Lord and you need to disappear so that in this land many souls in love with God may sprout. Dream and reality will surpass your dreams. The plant is beginning to sprout and then it will grow. . . . Will there be difficulties? Inevitably. God always blesses with the Cross. But together with personal or collective difficulties, we will have the grace of God to overcome them and to shout with joy, 'Lord, here I am because you have called me!'"

Forming His Daughters and Sons

To the very end of his life, del Portillo worked at transmitting to his sons and daughters the spirit of the founder. He frequently preached to the members of the general council during their morning half hour of mental prayer. Every week he gave them a practical class on the spirit of the Work.

His concern to form the members of the Work was not limited to those closest to him. In the weeks immediately following his election as president general, he directed a relatively short letter and another much longer one to all members, stressing fidelity to the legacy of the founder and asking for prayers. From then on, he frequently wrote messages to all the members—sometimes Christmas greetings, other times news of events like the opening of the founder's process of beatification, and from time to time noting anniversaries such as Escrivá's death or events in the history of Opus Dei. Some of these letters were quite short, but the letter he wrote on the occasion of the beatification of the founder, a detailed program of fidelity to his spirit built around a meditation on the mysteries of the Rosary, was almost 100 printed pages. Even longer is his letter for the fiftieth anniversary of the founding of the Priestly Society of the Holy Cross; it examines in detail two essential characteristics of the vocation to Opus Dei: priestly soul and lay mentality.

In the first decade after Escrivá's death, del Portillo's letters to the members were normally triggered by specific events. In February 1984, however, he began to write a monthly letter on the first of each month. Those letters, normally four single-spaced pages, often contained reflections on upcoming Church feasts and anniversaries of events in the life of Opus Dei. The aim was to help members deepen their interior life and improve their apostolic activities. Invariably, they ended with a request for prayers for himself and his intentions. In March 1984, for instance, he wrote, "Before God I feel like a poor fellow with empty hands. I beseech you not to deprive me of the charity of your daily prayer for me and for my intentions." Between 1975 and his death in 1994, del Portillo wrote 176 pastoral letters that cover almost 1,500 printed pages.

His pastoral letters reflect a keen awareness of the challenges facing people who wish to live as serious Christians in a time of pervasive consumerism, hedonism, and relativism. In a 1985 letter he warned: "A wave of hedonism, of unrestrained search for pleasure of every sort, is spreading throughout the entire world among rich and poor, men and women, young people, old people, and even children. With the grace of God we have to give our colleagues, friends, and relatives a firm and generous testimony of fortitude and temperance, of austerity in the use of the goods of this earth and of sobriety in food and drink. The authenticity of our vocation and the reality of our service to the Church are at stake."

In this context, he singled out spending too much time watching television. "I have insisted a great deal, and I will

continue to insist, that you need to choose very well what
television programs to see. Even more, we have to overcome
the almost morbid dependence on television that many people feel . . . For a person who has to sanctify himself by
working, it is absurd to waste time, which belongs to God,
watching television programs every day. Let me suggest the
possibility of offering another small mortification to the
Lord, going against our own tastes and what we may be
tempted to justify easily with the false and deceptive excuse
that it is a very generalized custom."

He underlined the need for fortitude and daring in the
apostolate, particularly in places where taking Christ's message seriously might be viewed by some people as fanaticism:
"You are afraid to be demanding, because some people will
go away. Inevitably some will go away, but if you are not
demanding you will never achieve anything."

The point on which he most insisted, however, was charity, love of neighbor. Shortly before his death, he wrote:
"May you love each other more each day. Do not become
tired of serving each other. May you lay down your lives
for each other to the point of acquiring a psychological pre-
disposition of thinking always about others. What do they
need? What are they interested in? What do they like? We
cannot allow the family warmth of our homes to grow cold
even in the smallest degree."

CHAPTER 16

SERVING OPUS DEI
AND THE CHURCH

D el Portillo's tenure coincided with difficult years in the
life of the Church. It was a time of institutional con-
traction and frequent controversy in many places. Despite
this unfavorable environment, however, Opus Dei continued
to expand numerically, geographically, and in the range of its
apostolic activities.

Growth and Expansion

The Work grew from 60,000 members at the founder's death
to 78,000 at del Portillo's death. Some 800 members were
ordained priests during the same time. Numerical growth was
accompanied by geographic expansion. When Don Alvaro
succeeded Escrivá, Opus Dei had centers in thirty-two countries. It was present in most of Western Europe and North and
South America as well as in Australia and a small number of
countries in Africa and Asia. During the nineteen years that del
Portillo governed Opus Dei, it began stable apostolic activities
in twenty new countries: Bolivia (1978), Honduras, Zaire (now
called Democratic Republic of Congo), and Ivory Coast (1980),
Hong Kong (1981), Singapore (1982), Trinidad-Tobago (1983),
Sweden (1984), Taiwan (1985), Finland (1987), Cameroon
and the Dominican Republic (1988), Macau, New Zealand,

and Poland (1989), Czechoslovakia and Hungary (1990), Nicaragua (1992), and Israel and India (1993).

At his time of del Portillo's death, Lithuania was preparing to join the list. For some years, members of the Work from the United States had conducted summer camps in that country featuring the study of English. A number of parents who had gotten to know the Work this way would welcome the first members when they moved there in fall 1994. As a reminder to pray for the beginning of the apostolate of Opus Dei in that country, Don Alvaro kept on his desk a picture of Our Lady of the Dawn Gate, the most venerated image of the Blessed Virgin in Lithuania. At the urging of St. John Paul II, he was also beginning to lay the foundations for starting Opus Dei in Kazakhstan.

Del Portillo actively promoted this geographic expansion. While others at times thought lack of people and money counseled moving more slowly, his zeal and determination were for forging ahead.

The practice in a new country began with visits by members from some nearby country to meet people and, with the permission of the local bishop, to organize days of recollection, retreats, and other formational activities. Often, too, one or more married members would already be there due to their jobs.

When it was time to start the first center, del Portillo would invite a group of half a dozen people—priests and laymen—to move there. The group would be made up of people from different countries to avoid their becoming an isolated foreign clique. Following the policy of Escrivá, del Portillo urged rapid adaptation to the new environment—learning the language, adopting the customs, and above all thinking of themselves not as foreigners but as newly minted natives.

Shortly before their departure for the new country, he invited them to Rome for a few days. During their stay he spoke with each one, spent time with the group in informal meetings, and preached to them. This exposure to his faith and optimism was part of their preparation for what would often be a difficult task.

Style of Government

First as Opus Dei's president general and later as its prelate, del Portillo headed what Escrivá like to describe as "a small part of the Church," but which was actually a sizeable international organization. Among the most important of the many different tasks this involved were setting overall direction and goals within the broad framework of Opus Dei's spirit, transmitting that spirit to the members, interpreting and applying it in changing circumstances, and maintaining and building the sense of family, with its twin components of fraternity among members and filiation between members and himself as the Father. He also had to make decisions about concrete issues like allocating human and financial resources to specific apostolic tasks and deciding which members to call to the priesthood.

Escrivá had established that in Opus Dei several people should study matters before decisions are taken. Del Portillo followed this rule, seeking the advice of others before making decisions. Someone who worked with him recalled: "His welcoming attitude meant that no one failed to express his opinions or the doubts or questions he might have for fear of looking bad or making a mistake. . . . He did not cling to his own opinions. He knew how to rectify whenever necessary. . . . He created around him an environment of confidence and freedom. But above all, he governed Opus Dei with affection, with the closeness to each soul that is so typical of an authentic pastor."

At the same time, he did not hesitate to correct and rebuke when necessary. For instance, if a response to a question or request from one of the regions was delayed unnecessarily, the person responsible was likely to hear: "You can't let yourself forget about the paperwork. There's nothing more disheartening than administrative silence." But it was done with tact, without raising his voice and in a pleasant manner. Once it was said, he forgot it, and showed the same confidence and affection as before.

The father of a family once asked him how to combine strength with affection in raising children. His response can be taken as a description of his approach to governing: "Just let them see a smile on your face. . . . When you have to correct them, don't put on a long face. Say with a smile whatever needs to be said, and don't worry. When people know that you really love them, you can tell them anything, no matter how painful."

He also asked his collaborators to practice "a demandingness that is full of affection, full of the respect and gentleness that our Father asked of us in our treatment of others—but at the same time really demanding. We have to call a spade a spade. If we don't, we're not fulfilling our obligations."

He created an atmosphere of calm cooperation. A collaborator recalls him as having "great organizational capabilities and a special gift for stimulating teamwork. He lived a patient urgency that created around him a calm focused effort. Working with him, one advanced quickly but with enormous tranquility, without wasting one's effort in agitation."

Seeing Souls Behind the Papers

Following Escrivá's practice of studying and resolving most matters in writing, with only a few brief meetings, del Portillo spent many hours at his desk reviewing dossiers typically containing a written statement of an issue, a solution or approach recommended by a member of the General Council, written comments by other members of the General Council and their staff, and a final recommendation.

Despite all the paperwork, he always tried to focus on the persons whom his decisions would affect. Each question was treated as if it were the only one he faced. On one occasion he said: "Every day I receive piles of dossiers. I don't skim them. I study everything slowly in the presence of God, doing everything possible to make the right decision, because I know very well what our Father taught us so often, that behind the papers there are souls."

Del Portillo did not complain about how much work he had to do. A clue can be found, however, in the time it took to publish some of the books Escrivá had left not quite finished at his death. *Friends of God* was published in 1977 and *The Way of the Cross* in 1981, but *Furrow* did not see the light of day until 1986 and *Forge* until 1987. In addition, ten years went by between the founder's death and completion of the annotations Escrivá had asked del Portillo to write for the notebooks called his *Apuntes íntimos*. In many cases Don Alvaro was the only person who knew the background. If he were to die without having completed the annotations, no one else could do so equally well. When he finally finished, he commented, "That's a load off my mind! I had that command from the Father weighing on me, but in all these years I couldn't carry it out."

Apostolic Activities

In countries where Opus Dei was already present, del Portillo urged the members and directors to advance the apostolate as quickly as possible to new areas and new types of activities. Unlike many ecclesiastical institutions specializing in, say, education or healthcare, Opus Dei seeks to help people sanctify themselves in their own jobs and social settings,

whatever these might be. Often, along with personal apostolate with friends, family members, colleagues, and neigh-
bors, this means joining others to create and run institutions
to address social, educational, or cultural issues of their
society while transmitting the spirit of Christ. In some cases,
Opus Dei takes official responsibility for the Christian
formation offered there, and these institutions engage in
"corporate" apostolates. Most activities, however, are
simply personal undertakings. Del Portillo urged members
to be creative in initiating both corporate apostolates and
personal undertakings.

Social Works

Don Alvaro focused particularly on activities designed to
alleviate poverty and suffering. In 1981 he wrote: "All of
us have to make contact with those who are suffering, who
are sick, who are destitute, who are alone, who have been
forsaken by all." In them, he added, are found "our riches
enabling us to work harder; our treasure, enabling us to
fall more deeply in love with God and to grow stronger in
our vocation; our strength, the strength of God, enabling
us to conquer."

During a trip to Mexico in 1983, he told a large group of
members of Opus Dei and cooperators: "My children, traveling through various parts of the country, I have noted a great
difference between the social classes. I see rich people who
are too rich and poor people who are too poor. Recalling
the teaching of the Apostle St. John, I say to everyone that it
is not true that we love God if we do not love our neighbor
whom we have close to us and see." Privately he urged the
directors and members of Opus Dei to devise new corporate
activities to contribute to solving social problems. The years
that followed saw the launching of the Jarales Professional

School in Guadalajara and the Center of Technical and Industrial Studies and Formation in a particularly poor area north of Mexico City to provide desperately needed educational options for working class youths.

Similarly, during a visit to the Philippines, he was struck by the poverty, especially in the city of Cebu, and he urged members of the Work to lend a hand to help young people. Within a few years, members of Opus Dei and their friends had started technical training schools in the poorest neighborhoods of Cebu and Manila.

These were not isolated examples. With del Portillo's support and urging, in countries from Argentina to Kenya members of Opus Dei, together with many cooperators and friends, began social service projects ranging from agricultural schools to centers that specialized in training women for the hospitality industry. As an indirect but effective way of serving the poor, del Portillo also encouraged the development of business schools that not only would equip their graduates with technical skills but would motivate them to serve their communities by creating jobs, training workers, and producing quality products at a fair price.

There was an emphasis, too, on social projects that responded to the specific needs of particular areas. In the late 1980s in the Democratic Republic of Congo, for example, Don Alvaro encouraged and supported members of Opus Dei who were involved in planning and developing a walk-in clinic in a very poor area on the outskirts of the capital where no medical services were available. During his visit to Kinshasa in 1989, the president of the bishops' conference told him that because of the lack of quality medical care in the country and the close links of the Social Security system with the one in Belgium, it was customary for religious and priests to go to Belgium for treatment even of relatively minor ailments, a practice both expensive and disruptive.

Could the members of the Work develop the clinic they were building into a full-scale modern facility which would offer to people of all social strata high enough quality healthcare to obviate the need to go to Belgium? The Work had been in the Congo for less than a decade and still had a relatively small presence. Nevertheless, del Portillo passed on the suggestion, and the doctors took up the challenge.

They started with a walk-in clinic, called Monkole, in one of the poorest neighborhoods on the outskirts of Kishasa. Although the country suffered devastating civil wars (1996–1997 and 1998–2003), by 2014 Monkole had grown into a fifty-five-bed hospital center with specialized departments for neonatal and pediatric medicine and treatment of AIDS, a school of nursing, and a training center for health aides. It is one of the largest and most modern medical centers in Congo, with plans well along for expanding to 150 beds.

Monkole is still located in a poor neighborhood on the outskirts of the capital and offers low-cost care at its central location and outpatient centers in three other poor neighborhoods. The quality of care, however, attracts not only the poor but members of the diplomatic corps, employees of foreign companies and not-for-profit organizations, and religious and clergy. Their fees make it possible to offer high quality care to the many patients who cannot pay. The medical director likes to describe this as a "Robin Hood" system.

Education

Education was another priority area for del Portillo. Along with giving young men and women an excellent education, he wanted them to be prepared to be good parents, good citizens, and good Catholics. This involved setting up new schools and developing existing ones in many countries, with parents very much part of the team. Following Escrivá's lead, del Portillo insisted that a school focus first on families, then on teachers, and finally on the students. He urged schools drawing students from upper- and upper-middle class families to establish generous scholarship programs for children from poor families.

Only a small percentage of these schools were corporate activities of Opus Dei, but they shared many characteristics derived from its spirit, including an emphasis on freedom, a desire for academic excellence, and concern for the integral development—including religious development—of the students.

At the time of Escrivá's death, three universities existed that were corporate activities of Opus Dei: the University of Navarre in Pamplona, Spain, the Pan-American University with campuses in Mexico City, Guadalajara, and Aguascalientes, and the University of Piura in Peru. Del Portillo realized the need for such institutions to do serious research, not least to "demonstrate that belief in God does not paralyze or block reason, the capacity to know reality and to advance human life." As grand chancellor of the University of Navarre, he accordingly promoted the creation of the Center of Applied Medical Research. As a world-class research center, this would require investments of personnel and money well beyond what the university had available, but del Portillo insisted, and partnerships with national and international pharmaceutical and medical device companies eventually provided the resources. More than 300 scientists and physicians now do research there, focusing on genetic therapy, hepatology, cardiovascular science, oncology, and neurosciences.

With del Portillo's encouragement and support, new universities were founded in Colombia, Argentina, Chile, and the Philippines. He was especially closely involved in the project for a university-level institution in Rome specializing in biomedical sciences. Despite a legal climate in Italy unfavorable to private universities, members of the Work, together with friends and colleagues in the medical field, managed to launch an institution in Rome that includes a medical school, a university hospital, a nursing school, and a school of biomedical and chemical engineering.

None of these educational institutions is "Catholic" in the sense of being promoted by the hierarchy. Professional educators created them and run them. But these schools are imbued with a Christian spirit that places them at the service of the Church. When addressing the faculty of any of them, del Portillo insisted on the importance of teaching "as Christians." Even those in technical fields should not to leave their Christian convictions behind upon entering the classroom, he routinely said.

Ecclesial Service

Del Portillo also promoted a number of institutions that serve the needs of the Church directly. Since the 1950s Escrivá had dreamed of opening a university in Rome where priests from all over the world could study philosophy, theology, canon law, and other ecclesiastical subjects, with encouragement to lead a deep interior life of prayer and sacrifice and grow in their sense of union with the Holy Father and the Church everywhere.

In 1983 del Portillo decided to take steps toward making these dreams a reality by establishing what would become the Pontifical University of the Holy Cross. The project was daunting. In recent decades, the number of priestly and religious vocations had declined sharply and with it the number of potential students. Rome already had a large number of pontifical universities and other institutions, some with centuries of tradition and great prestige. Assembling a faculty, acquiring appropriate space, and finding students would require an enormous effort. Said del Portillo: "We cannot allow ourselves to be moved by a false objectivity which would lead us to focus on the difficulties . . . and forget that on the other side of the balance is the grace of God which is more powerful."

Simply obtaining permission to start a new university was not easy. Del Portillo decided to move forward on a temporary basis by having the program in Rome sponsored by the ecclesiastical schools of the University of Navarre. The problem of finding space was solved through an agreement with the Holy See, allowing the new institution to rent the Palazzo dell'Appolinare, a large historic building in central Rome near the Piazza Navona.

The Roman Academic Center of the Holy Cross opened in 1984 with forty students. Six years later, it received the rank of a pontifical athenaeum, and in 1998 John Paul II designated it a pontifical university. By 2013 the school had 1,020 full-time students from eighty-one countries. About 460 students came from Europe, 157 from Central and South America, 137 from Canada, the United States, and Mexico (eighty-three from the U.S.), 121 from Asia, 109 from Africa, and six from Oceania.

At the request of Pope John Paul, del Portillo also created two international seminaries, one in Pamplona, Spain (1988) and one in Rome (1991). Besides providing a home for young men studying for the priesthood in the school of theology at the University of Navarre and at the Pontifical University of the Holy Cross, the seminaries are centers of formation for future priests from dioceses across the world. Bidasoa, in Spain, at this time has 100 students from forty-six dioceses in fourteen countries; Sedes Sapientiae, in Rome, has eighty-six students from fifty-eight dioceses in twenty-seven countries.

In the years immediately following the fall of the Communist regimes in Central and Eastern Europe, del Portillo was especially interested in making it possible for priests and seminarians from those countries to study in Rome. Since the impoverished state of the Church in those countries meant students would require substantial financial assistance, del Portillo spearheaded the creation of an international foundation to raise money for this purpose. At this time a large percentage of students from Central and Eastern Europe, Africa, and South America receive scholarships covering a large portion of their tuition and living expenses.

Personal Service to the Church

Escrivá's frequently repeated statements that Opus Dei exists to serve the Church inspired not only the focus del Portillo gave to Opus Dei's activities but also his personal activity. Despite the heavy demands involved in heading Opus Dei, he served in various capacities in the Vatican—consultor of the Congregation for the Doctrine of the Faith until 1983, consultor of the Congregation for the Causes of Saints from 1982 on, and consultor of the Pontifical Council for Social Communications from 1984 on. His most time-consuming position, however, was as consultor of the Commission for the Revision of the Code of Canon law, for which he served on four study groups and prepared numerous reports, some quite lengthy.

St. John Paul II also asked him to participate in three assemblies of the world synod of bishops. At the 1987 synod on the vocation and mission of the laity, he spoke about the universal call to sanctity, the secular nature of the laity's mission, and the need for ecclesial communion. During the synod on the formation of priests, he delivered an address on the priest as "Minister of the Church, Servant of Men." One of those who served with him described his interventions as models of "lucidity, respect, and . . . adherence to the Magisterium of the Church."

Love for the Church

Del Portillo welcomed the emergence of new groups to serve the Church, saying it meant that "many other people will draw closer to God." This welcoming attitude was reflected in his relations with the Communion and Liberation movement founded by Msgr. Luigi Giussani. As a way of showing support at a time when that group was having difficulties in certain Italian ecclesiastical circles, del Portillo twice invited Msgr. Giussani to dinner at the headquarters of Opus Dei and also participated in a round table Giusanni organized. In a letter to del Portillo, Giusanni wrote: "The exquisite and operative charity with which you always deal with us is a motive and example of edification. It makes us hope to continue to receive your advice and support."

Don Alvaro's love for the Church and his theological appreciation for the role of bishops led him to pray for them and try to support them. A few months before the assassination of Bishop Oscar Romero of El Salvador, del Portillo wrote to him: "I assure you that I will pray for you daily at holy Mass, for you and for all the work of souls you carry out." When visiting cathedrals and shrines of Our Lady, he often sent postcards to friends in the hierarchy assuring them of his prayer and affection. Many recipients commented on how much good this simple token of friendship had done them.

Del Portillo also urged Opus Dei's members, friends, and cooperators to be closely united to their local bishop. In a letter to some young men who were about to be ordained, he wrote in 1976: "Always stay very united to the Roman Pontiff, the common Father of the faithful, the Vicar of Christ on earth—the 'Vice-Christ' as our Father so lovingly used to call him. And in each diocese be very united to the bishop, showing him deep affection and great respect. Remember the immense love, both theological and human, which our beloved founder had for the diocesan bishops."

In his many meetings with diocesan priests, he urged them to pray daily for their bishop's intentions and to see him as a father who needed their affection and close collaboration. Often he reminded them of a phrase of St. Cyprian, "*Nihil sine espiscopo*"—"Nothing without the bishop."

Don Alvaro had great esteem and affection for religious orders and congregations and felt special affection for the members of contemplative communities. He was delighted to have them pray for Opus Dei. Once when someone spoke to him about the "power" of Opus Dei, he answered, "Yes, we have a great weapon that few know about, the prayer of so many cloistered monasteries all over the world that pray for us. This is our weapon."

He urged the members of Opus Dei to pray for "cloistered religious who are a great treasure for the Church. Pray that they may have many vocations and that they may be very holy." On a number of occasions, he sought contributions for convents with special needs. He also supported the beatification cause of a number of nuns, principally Discalced Carmelites, including Edith Stein—today, St. Teresa Benedicta of the Cross.

He personally helped a number of religious orders solve problems they encountered in following the mandate of Vatican II to adapt to new conditions while remaining faithful to their foundational charism. A particularly striking case is his support of what would become the Daughters of Holy Mary of the Heart of Jesus.

In the late 1970s and early 1980s, Mother María de Jesús Velarde, the superior of the Spanish province of the

Daughters of Our Lady of the Sacred Heart, a congregation founded in France in the nineteenth century, became convinced that the only way the Spanish convents could remain faithful to their charism and retain their unity and vitality was by becoming independent. She first received help and guidance from her confessor, Fr. Jesús Solano, SJ.

After his death she was introduced to Don Alvaro, who offered his assistance. Over the course of nine years, she met with him thirty-six times, usually for about an hour. In addition, she spoke with him by telephone more than 100 times, and received a dozen letters from him. Thanks in large part to Don Alvaro's support, in 1998, the Holy See transformed the Spanish province into a new congregation the Daughters of Holy Mary of the Heart of Jesus. It is now active in Rome, the United States, Mexico, Guatemala, El Salvador, Peru, Argentina, and Chile as well as Spain.

On the fiftieth anniversary of Opus Dei, del Portillo described "love for the Holy Church as a central aspect of its spirit." One of his closest collaborators once asked him if he should accept a position that would be a service to the Church but very time-consuming. Don Alvaro's answer, "Always say yes," reflects his own approach throughout his life.

CHAPTER 17

REACHING OUT TO CROWDS

From the beginning del Portillo saw informal get-to-gethers with small numbers of people ("tertualias") as an important way for him as the Father to communicate Opus Dei's spirit. In the final years of his life, however, the founder had also had informal get-togethers with large groups, starting with students who came to Rome at Easter for the international student congresses known as UNIV and eventually including encounters with throngs in auditoriums or outdoor venues during his catechetical trips to Spain and Latin America.

There were powerful reasons for continuing this tradition, but at first del Portillo did not think that he could. The founder had been gifted with an extraordinarily warm voice and outgoing personality that enabled him to connect with people on a one-on-one basis even though thousands were present. Although warm and caring, his successor was by temperament much less outgoing—indeed, somewhat shy and retiring—and although he spoke well, he did not have Escrivá's literary and poetic gifts or his sense of timing and dramatic flair.

Despite his misgivings, the members of the General Council urged him to continue the tradition of meeting the students from Opus Dei centers around the world who came to Rome at Easter to see the Holy Father and participate in

UNIV. Agreeing, del Portillo said, "I won't do the work. It will be the Holy Spirit who works in souls." Though in some ways very different in style and tone from Escrivá's, Don Alvaro's meetings with the students had the intimate warmth of a family reunion. The young people sensed his genuine interest and affection and responded in kind. Said one, "I felt like the Father was speaking to me alone, in private, looking straight into my heart and communicating to me all the depth and demandingness of his own life." Members of Opus Dei came away from the get-togethers with a stronger sense of the Work as a family, while non-members often made resolutions to improve their lives as Christians, and some discovered their vocation to Opus Dei or other forms of apostolic service.

Apostolic Journeys

Although still believing he lacked the natural gifts needed for talking with large numbers of people, the results of the UNIV meetings confirmed del Portillo in his belief that the Holy Spirit would make up for what he lacked. "The important thing," he told listeners, "is not what I can say but what the Holy Spirit makes each one of you hear in the depths of your heart. The Sanctifier acts if we let him, and with his action transforms our souls." Don Alvaro now decided that he should continue the tradition established by Escrivá of traveling to different countries to meet with as many people as possible in informal settings. For the rest of his life, such trips would form an important part of his schedule.

It was natural that he traveled much more frequently in Europe than elsewhere. Some of the European visits were prolonged, but most were relatively short trips during which he concentrated on visiting Opus Dei centers and meeting with members, with perhaps one or two larger meetings at some other venue.

His trips outside Europe involved prolonged stays and many meetings with large groups of people. Several were to countries of the Americas. The first, in 1983, was centered on visiting the sanctuary of Our Lady of Guadalupe to give thanks to the Virgin for Opus Dei's recognition as a prelature. On the way to Mexico, he stopped for two days in Canada, but most of his time was spent in Mexico, where he stayed from April 27 to May 23.

On the second day of his novena of thanksgiving in the Basilica of Guadalupe, the abbot of the basilica invited him to enter the small chamber where the image of Our Lady is housed and where visitors can kiss the glass that covers it. Deeply moved, del Portillo kissed the hands and feet of the image, but said he considered himself unworthy to kiss the face. After Father Echevarría reminded him that Mary is our Mother, del Portillo kissed her lovingly on the cheek.

Following the novena, he had get-togethers with thousands of people in Mexico City and other parts of the country. He also found time to meet personally with people who had special needs. The first was a member of the Work who was paralyzed and unable to speak due to a brain tumor. Del Portillo greeted him saying, "Your eyes express that you love God, that you love the Work, that you love the Father, that you love your brothers. . . . I remember you every day. I pray for you every day. We need each other mutually. I need you and you need me." At the end of the visit, having told the man to be very cheerful and serene, he added: "I realize that you are. I read in your eyes your love for God, your love for the vocation, your love of the Father." Then del Portillo kissed him on the forehead, saying he was kissing the Holy Cross.

On the day he left Mexico, del Portillo paid a final visit to Our Lady of Guadalupe. He prayed aloud: "As you remember, little Mother, our Father came to petition you. We have come to thank you. Our Father finished that novena before your image saying, 'Mother, I don't ask you for anything more because I know that you have listened to me; I am in your hands' You did listen to us, and we continue to be in your hands. In the name of the whole Work, in addition to thanking you, I ask you that we may be faithful. . . . Our Mother, look at us with those eyes of yours full of mercy. You are looking at us. We realize that. We feel it in the deepest part of our soul, and we love you very much."

After Mexico, he briefly visited Guatemala and Colombia, and at the very end of the trip, New York. There he met Cardinal Cooke, prayed in St. Patrick's Cathedral, and spoke with members and friends of Opus Dei. Noting that the United States exercises enormous influence for both good and evil, he illustrated the point by recounting that on a recent trip to Poland he had observed the effects not only of the atheistic materialism imposed by the communist regime but also of the practical materialism reflected in the behavior of American tourists. "I come to tell you, with all my affection, that you should react," he said. "All of you have to be leaven to ferment the mass so that this great American nation may become the good bread of Christ."

During this first trip to countries of the Americas, he spoke with more than 150 groups, ranging in size from a handful to several thousand. It was a grueling trip for a man almost seventy years old and in rather poor health, but del Portillo appeared to draw energy from its spiritual fruits: conversions, greater seriousness in the practice of the faith, and vocations to dedicate one's entire life to God.

* * *

In 1987 del Portillo spent more than a month visiting Asia and Oceania. Many participants in get-togethers in

Singapore, Hong Kong, Taiwan, Korea, and Japan were not
Christians. Del Portillo spoke with them with great affection,
often expressing his admiration for their natural virtues,
while stressing his faith in Christ and in the Church. In Tai-
pei, for instance, he commended the dedication to work that
had produced an economic miracle, as well as the hospitality and other virtues he had observed. But he also expressed
hope that "the light of Christ—which is the only true light—
will reach all the people of this great country."

* * *

His longest catechetical journey, lasting from January 17
to March 11, 1988, was to Canada, the United States, and
Puerto Rico, with a brief side trip to Mexico (primarily to
revisit the shrine of Our Lady of Guadalupe). In the US he
visited virtually every city where Opus Dei had a center:
Boston, New York, Washington, Miami, Houston, Los Angeles, San Francisco, Chicago, St. Louis, Milwaukee, and Pitts-
burgh. Even under the best of circumstances, the trip would
have been long and exhausting, but traveling in Canada
and in the American Midwest in the middle of winter added
snowstorms that at times threatened to close highways and
airports. Del Portillo took it all in stride.

In Boston, del Portillo remarked that upon seeing the
campuses of Harvard and MIT he was tempted to ask himself what Opus Dei, with its limited means, could possibly do
in such an environment. Then he recalled Escrivá's experience in London in 1958, when, seeing the wealth and power
accumulated in its great banks and international businesses,
he thought, "I just can't"—and the Lord responded, "You
can't, but I can."

"What are we going to do?" del Portillo asked. "We have
to make an effort to be salt and leaven so that those who
make up these powerful institutions can draw closer to God

and have more Christian spirit. In that way, we will do a great service to this nation and to the entire world."

Recurring topics during the trip were family and openness to children. In Los Angeles he addressed the question of putting off the birth of children for financial reasons, suggesting that the issue arises mostly in wealthy countries. And he urged his audience: "I ask you to spread everywhere the true doctrine of the Church, that it is not licit to stop up the wellsprings of life, to use contraceptives."

Perhaps because of America's size and influence, he seems to have insisted more than usual on the need for many vocations. Asked in Chicago what his favorite aspiration was, he answered, "Seeing this immense city and this immense country, a very good aspiration is what our Father wrote in *The Way*: 'Jesus, souls! Apostolic souls! They are for you, for your glory.'"

* * *

Del Portillo's last major trips were to Africa, where he spent more than thirty days during 1989. His precarious health and the difficulties in getting from one country to another led him to make four separate trips, returning to Rome after each: Kenya from April 1 to April 10; Zaire and Cameroon from August 22 to August 30; Ivory Coast from October 14 to October 19; and Nigeria from November 9 to November 20.

In Nairobi his induction as an elder included the presentation of a goat along with a shield and lance symbolic of the elder's role of protecting his people, and a fly whisk representing the elder's duty to open a path for those who come after him. At the beginning of the first large get-together in Nairobi, encouraging his listeners to be daring in their interior life and apostolate, he quoted a Kenyan proverb: "There are no mountains on the path to the home of a loved one."

In Kenya and the other African countries he visited, del Portillo insisted on the need to work to eliminate poverty and overcome divisions among races and tribe. "We have to understand and love everyone. If we have received more goods from God, we have to use them to help our brothers who are in need. While it is natural to have special affection for members of the same tribe and nation," he said, "we must build a supernatural reality on this human one. Belonging to a specific tribe should not separate us from others. Belonging to a tribe is a reality, but over and above it we have to place Christ. Then our heart will expand and all tribes will fit within it."

Del Portillo also insisted on the high hopes for Africa held by the Holy Father and himself. "The Pope expects a great deal from you," he said. "You are the continent of the future, but it is necessary to give more to the Lord."

In the years after Escrivá's death, del Portillo visited more than three dozen countries and spoke with hundreds of thousands of people of different ages, cultures, and social conditions. He once remarked: "For me, one day of working in Rome is much harder than a whole year of preaching in all these different places. It is such a joy to come into contact with so many souls and to see how God stirs them up and draws them to himself." There is no doubt that he meant it. But intercontinental travel and the strain of speaking several times a day before large audiences took a serious toll. By the end of his last African trip, del Portillo was seventy-five years old and in delicate health. He would continue to travel extensively in Europe virtually to the end of his life, but he was no longer strong enough to undertake intercontinental journeys.

CHAPTER 18

FRIEND OF GARDENERS AND POPES

Although somewhat retiring by temperament, del Portillo had a natural gift for friendship and understood that being someone's friend could help that person become better friends with Christ. Nor were his friendships passing affairs. Friendships he had made as a student, as an army officer, as an engineer, and as a young priest in many cases lasted the rest of his life.

All sorts of people were his friends. During the decade Villa Tevere was under construction, Don Alvaro was in close contact with Leonardo Castelli, owner of the construction company. Del Portillo was a demanding client, unwilling to overlook even relatively minor mistakes. Nonetheless, he became a close friend of Castelli and his family, and he served as an advisor and spiritual guide. Once when del Portillo was hospitalized, the whole Castelli family came to visit him, and Leonardo insisted on paying for his hospital stay. When Leonardo himself was diagnosed with a fatal illness, the family asked del Portillo to anoint him.

During a visit to the Cathedral of Notre Dame in Paris, he ran into a young African with whom he had a brief conversation. The young man began to correspond with del Portillo and sometime later decided to become a priest. Today, a pastor in Canada, he has on the wall of his office a photo of Don Alvaro, whom he addresses affectionately as "Papa."

Del Portillo's friends included many people whose work brought them into contact with him. The doorman of the building where the Castelli family lived made a point of calling his wife, children, and grandchildren to greet Don Alvaro when he was leaving the building. The man who made his cassocks for many years came with his wife and daughter to his wake; they recalled how he encouraged them to love God and speak of him with the people they met. Doormen and other Vatican employees would go out of their way to greet him if they saw him on the street, even after they retired.

Manolo, the gardener at a conference center where del Portillo spent several months over a period of years, said he felt part of Don Alvaro's family. On his first day on the job, del Portillo told him who he was and gave him a hug even though he was sweaty from work. "He talked with me as though I were someone he'd known all his life," the gardener recalled. When Manolo contracted a serious illness, del Portillo prayed for him every day, and every time he saw him, he asked how he was doing and what his doctors had to say. After del Portillo's death, Manolo said, "Now more than ever I look upon him as a friend, and I ask him for many things."

Until the end of his life, he counted among his friends the specialist who treated Escrivá for diabetes, even though his many eccentricities and lack of social graces made conversation with him difficult, if not downright unpleasant. As the years went by, more and more of his friends dropped him. Finally only Don Alvaro would invite him for dinner or accept his invitations, and there listen patiently to his theories.

During the Second Vatican Council, del Portillo made friends with a host of bishops and council experts. Many stayed in touch with him for the rest of their lives. The Canadian Cardinal Edouard Gagnon wrote: "The esteem and gratitude which I have felt toward Bishop Alvaro del Portillo from when we first met has grown over time and become authentic veneration. Back then our meetings did a great deal of good for my spiritual life. Today the memory of this exemplary pastor is a source of inspiration for me . . . I have always felt small in his presence but also strengthened, because he reminded me that God carries out the greatest works using the smallest of men." Preaching at a memorial Mass for Bishop del Portillo, Cardinal Law of Boston said, "I often enjoyed his hospitality in Rome. He was extraordinarily affectionate. Whenever I was with him, I always had the feeling that I was one of the family."

Friend of Popes

Anecdotes of del Portillo's friendships with all sorts of people could fill a book, but now we will turn to his friendship with popes.

From the very beginning of Opus Dei, Escrivá prayed fervently, and taught the members to pray, an aspiration that he incorporated into *The Way*: "*Omnes cum Petro ad Iesum per Mariam*" (Everyone with Peter to Jesus through Mary). Union with the Pope, whoever he might be, is central to the spirit of Opus Dei, but Don Alvaro's dealings with popes, particularly in the case of John Paul II, also reflected warm personal friendships.

Upon succeeding Escrivá as head of Opus Dei, del Portillo's friendship with Pope Paul VI already went back thirty-two years to their first meeting in Rome in 1943. The relationship had taken on a new tone and meaning when Cardinal Montini became Pope in June 1963 and was transformed again when del Portillo became the head of the "little piece of the Church" that is Opus Dei.

At Escrivá's wake, the undersecretary of state, representing the Pope, told del Portillo that Paul VI had said he would be spiritually present, praying next to the body of "such a faithful son" of the Church and of the vicar of Christ. In a telegram, the secretary of state said the Holy Father was praying for the soul of the founder and sent his blessing to all the members of Opus Dei. In a letter thanking Pope Paul, del Portillo assured him that "before the tomb of our dearly beloved founder, all of us, Holy Father, renew our firm resolution to be very faithful to his spirit, and we also offer our lives for the Church and for the Pope."

Del Portillo's first audience as head of Opus Dei with Paul VI was on March 5, 1976, and lasted more than an hour. Del Portillo, who asked the Pope's permission to share some of the contents of the audience with the members of the Work, was overjoyed at hearing the Holy Father say he considered the founder of Opus Dei "one of the men in the history of the Church who had received the most charisms and who had responded with the greatest generosity to God's gifts." Pope Paul urged him to be sure to write down everything concerning Opus Dei's founder, calling it "a treasure, not only for Opus Dei, but for the whole Church."

Love for the Pope led del Portillo to share his intentions and his sufferings. Learning that Paul VI had found it necessary to suspend the French Archbishop Lefebvre for disobedience, he was deeply upset at the suffering this would cause the Pope and the harm it would do the Church. The next morning he sent a telegram to the secretary of state asking him to tell the Holy Father that Opus Dei was closely united to him and praying for him in these difficult circumstances. He repeated these sentiments a few days later in a letter.

For Paul VI's eightieth birthday in 1977 Don Alvaro sent him a copy of the first edition of *The Way* along with a warm letter. During Holy Week 1978, with Paul VI too ill to hold his usual Wednesday audience, del Portillo urged the several thousand university students in Rome for the UNIV conference to go to St. Peter's Square for the blessing the Pope would give from his window. Seeing so many young people was sure to cheer him up, Don Alvaro believed.

On June 19, 1978, he had another private audience with Pope Paul, once again lasting an hour. When the Holy Father asked him to pray at the founder's tomb for the Church and the Pope, he said he would do that as soon as he got back to Villa Tevere. "No," the Pope replied, "you have to eat first. Just do it sometime today."

In the days immediately preceding the conclave, a number of cardinals took advantage of being in Rome to meet with del Portillo because of his position as head of Opus Dei and also, in many cases, because they were friends of long standing. On August 16 Cardinal Wojtyla of Kraków, together with Bishop Andrzej Deskur of the Pontifical Council for Social Communication, joined del Portillo, Fr. Joaquin Alonso, and Fr. Javier Echevarría for dinner at Villa Tevere. Bishop Deskur, an intimate friend of del Portillo as well as of Wojtyla, had introduced them to each other during one of the sessions of the Second Vatican Council.

The following day, the dinner guest at Villa Tevere was Cardinal Luciani, Patriarch of Venice. Familiar with Opus Dei from its work in his diocese, he had published only a few weeks earlier a brief article about the founder of Opus Dei, whom he called a "revolutionary priest who vaulted over traditional barriers, pointing out mystical goals even to married people." Sometime earlier, del Portillo had asked several of his daughters to pray for Cardinal Luciani, adding, "What a good pope he would be!"

As they were making a visit to the Blessed Sacrament after dinner, del Portillo invited the patriarch to use a kneeler that had belonged to Pope Pius VII, elected pope in a conclave held in Venice in 1880. The kneeler later was acquired by Pope St. Pius X, who had been patriarch of Venice, and was given by his family to Opus Dei. As Cardinal Luciani knelt, del Portillo commented, "May this be an omen."

On the first day of the conclave, del Portillo visited a Marian shrine near Rome to pray for the future pope. The next day, as white smoke rose but before it was known who had been chosen, he dropped to his knees to pray for the new pope.

To the newly elected John Paul I he wrote: "A few days before your election to the papacy, I had the joy and the honor of telling Your Holiness personally that I and all the members of Opus Dei were praying very intensely for the future pope. In the same way now I assure Your Holiness that following the example and teaching of our founder of holy memory, we continue praying with the same intensity and constancy every day to God and to the Blessed Virgin Mary for you and for all your intentions."

Del Portillo was overjoyed at the election of Cardinal Luciani because he believed he was chosen by God to bring to an end the Church's years of trial, as well as because the new Pope thought very well of Opus Dei and its founder. Shortly after his election, John Paul I communicated unofficially to del Portillo that he wanted to solve the question of the Work's legal status and had instructed the Congregation for Religious to begin working on that.

The Pope's sudden death on September 28, only thirty-three days after his election, was a blow to del Portillo, who wept at the news though he was not given to tears. Once more he prayed for the deceased pontiff and his successor, asking members of the Work to offer "even our breathing so that the Holy Spirit may give us a Pope according to the Heart of Jesus Christ."

John Paul II

Del Portillo was overjoyed at the news that the cardinals had elected Cardinal Wojtyla, who chose the name John Paul II. The day after the election, Don Alvaro went to the hospital to visit Bishop Deskur, who had just suffered a serious stroke. As he left Deskur's room, he was astonished to encounter John Paul II, who had come to visit his friend, and delighted when the newly elected Pope gave him a warm embrace. Two days later, he visited the shrine of Our Lady of Mentorella outside of Rome, which he knew Cardinal Wojtyla had often visited, and from there sent a postcard to the Pope. Daily, he wrote, the faithful of Opus Dei offered thousands of Masses for the intentions of the head of Opus Dei—and his intentions were those of the Vicar of Christ. Several days later, he expanded on the same idea in a letter to John Paul II, adding, that "Opus Dei has no other will or desire than to be a good instrument in the hands of the Successor of Peter."

Moved by the postcard and the letter, John Paul II telephoned personally on October 27 to express thanks. Now and on other occasions when he spoke to the Holy Father by telephone, Don Alvaro knelt. Similarly, when he happened to encounter him in the Vatican Gardens, he knelt as he passed.

On October 28 John Paul II received del Portillo in an informal meeting which he called "a family reunion, not an audience." A few days later del Portillo, by then in Austria, wrote again, detailing the prayers and good works being offered for the Pope by the members of Opus Dei. A few weeks later, John Paul II again invited del Portillo to meet informally.

* * *

As Christmas drew near, del Portillo learned that it was customary in Poland to send oranges to relatives and friends
on the feast of Saint Nicholas. On that day, he personally
brought to the Pope some oranges, as well as a crozier
with an image of Our Lady of Czestochowa, some choco-
late Santa Claus figures, and several books by Escrivá. John
Paul II responded in kind, sending del Portillo on December
18 a basket of fruit and a photograph with a handwritten
blessing. Two days later he sent some Christmas cards with
his printed signature for distribution to members of Opus
Dei, and the following day a traditional Italian Christmas
cake, called a pannettone, arrived. On New Year's Day, John
Paul II invited Msgr. Alonso, one of del Portillo's two aides,
for dinner. During the meal the Pope offered a toast to the
Work, adding a prayer that in the year ahead God would
give it everything it needed.

Del Portillo was deeply moved by these signs of the
Pope's affection because, as he repeated frequently, he was
convinced that along with being the successor of St. Peter,
the new Pope was a saint. "Apart from the theological faith
which moves us to love the Vice-Christ," he told some
members, "John Paul II is so cordial, so good, so amiable,
that he wins the heart of all those who have any dealings
with him."

For his part, John Paul II appreciated del Portillo's
friendship, support, and pastoral zeal. One day at dinner
Don Alvaro talked about the importance of moving people to approach the sacrament of penance. Assenting with
a smile, John Paul II commented, "You remind me of the
good zealous pastors of my time who spent their lives
taking care in this way of the souls whom they loved with all
their strength."

Supporting the Pope

John Paul II quickly realized that he could count on Don Alvaro to support him with deeds as well as prayer and sacrifice. So, for instance, as the ordination in St. Peter's of his successor as Archbishop of Kraków approached, the Pope was concerned that the congregation, so far from Poland, might be embarrassingly small. He asked del Portillo to encourage members of Opus Dei in Rome to attend. Del Portillo did—and stayed away from the ceremony himself so that the members of the Work would pay attention to the new archbishop, not him.

John Paul II wanted to organize a special Mass for college students as a way of reaching out to the large number of young people studying in Rome's universities. The university chaplains said that they thought very few students would come, but del Portillo was enthusiastic and promised Opus Dei's wholehearted support. He suggested printing invitations that members of the Work and other students in touch with its apostolic activities could distribute among their classmates. He also offered the services of Opus Dei priests to hear confessions in St. Peter's for several hours before the Mass. The first university Mass was a complete success, with many students attending, and many taking advantage of the opportunity for confession.

The Pope later admitted that several hours before the event he'd begun looking out the window to see if anyone was coming. At first he was concerned that no buses were arriving, but after a while he began to see a steady stream of small groups of people, and by the time of Mass the basilica was full. From then on, John Paul II celebrated Mass twice a year for ever-growing numbers of university students.

John Paul II also wanted to organize a Corpus Christi procession through the streets of Rome for the first time in over a century. Once again, many people were skeptical. They doubted that the city would give permission and, even if it did, thought few people would take part. Del Portillo lent his enthusiastic support, not only urging members and friends of Opus Dei to attend but personally participating in the procession. Today it has become an annual Rome tradition.

In 1980, during an audience for students in Rome for the UNIV conference, one of them commented to John Paul II that he found St. Peter's Square incomplete because it had no image of the Blessed Virgin. Replied the Pope: "That's right! We should finish the square." A little later, del Portillo sent John Paul architectural sketches and photographs of a possible mosaic. There was no response until after the attempt on the Pope's life in May 1981. John Paul then determined to place an image of Mary in the square in thanksgiving for her protection, and del Portillo's proposal was approved. On December 8 the Pope blessed the large mosaic of Mary Mother of the Church that now overlooks the square. A few days later, he invited Don Alvaro to concelebrate Mass in his private chapel and join him for breakfast.

John Paul II made 147 foreign trips during his pontificate. Besides praying for their success himself, del Portillo encouraged the Opus Dei members in the countries the Pope would visit to pray and do all they could to ensure a warm welcome for him and his message. Especially where it appeared the welcome might not be so warm, del Portillo promoted visible—and audible—displays of affection for the Holy Father, like serenading him in the evening outside the place he was staying.

In 1989 del Portillo visited Sweden shortly before the Holy Father was due to arrive. In a public meeting with members, cooperators, and friends of Opus Dei, he urged them to "get many Catholics to go to confession so that they can understand better the Pope's message. But, you say, here almost no one goes to confession. Try to push them, feeling co-responsible for their salvation."

At times when the Pope found himself subject to criticism or attacks, del Portillo took special pains to assure him of his own support and that of Opus Dei. When the 1993 encyclical *Veritatis Splendor* on moral principles met with criticism, for instance, del Portillo published several articles explaining it and urged members of Opus Dei to support the encyclical. He also wrote John Paul, thanking him for the encyclical and attaching a number of positive articles.

Private Meetings

The friendship between the two men grew during the long years of the pontificate. They met frequently in formal audiences and much more frequently informally. When he was about to leave Rome, del Portillo often asked the Holy Father for a blessing for his trip and for the people he would see. John Paul invited him to concelebrate Mass and join him for meals. He also took note of special days in the life of Opus Dei. In 1989, for instance, he invited del Portillo for dinner on Escrivá's birthday. By one count, there were forty-eight meetings between the two in addition to Don Alvaro's participation in ceremonies or group meetings with the Pope. Greetings and small gifts from John Paul were not uncommon on Don Alvaro's birthday, and del Portillo often returned the favor on the Pope's birthday and significant anniversaries.

❋ ❋ ❋

Even so, del Portillo never took a casual view of being with the Holy Father, and he paid close attention to even his informal remarks. At dinner on Escrivá's birthday, for instance, John Paul II echoed Christ's command to "Go and bear fruit" (John 15:16), applying it specifically to Opus Dei.

Del Portillo immediately wrote to the members: "It is the command of Christ to the apostles and to all Christians, but the Pope directs it specifically to us. To go means to move, to get out of our egotism, to give ourselves to the others, to look for souls, to do apostolate. In this way we will fulfill the command of Christ which today has sounded once again in my ears pronounced by his vicar on this earth."

At the end of one of their meetings after he had been ordained a bishop, del Portillo asked John Paul to put on his bishop's ring for a moment. The Pope did, then returned the ring to its owner. Said Don Alvaro: "This ring helps me a great deal to be aware of the presence of God, because it is a symbol of my union with Opus Dei. It signifies that I am the slave, the servant of the Work for love of the Church and of the Pope. But now that Your Holiness has put it on, it will also contribute a lot to my being aware of the presence of the Pope." Later he told some members of the Work, "Before I prayed for him constantly, but now constantly multiplied many times over."

The Pope Shot

The attempt on the Pope's life in May 1981 was a terrible blow to del Portillo. He visited the hospital the same afternoon, even though he knew he could not see the Pope. He asked all members of Opus Dei to offer their Masses, Communions, and acts of mortification for the Holy Father. On May 19 he wrote the assistant secretary of state: "These days, in the midst of the pain we feel in our soul, the only thing we do is pray and pray to our Lord and to the Most Holy Virgin, for our beloved Holy Father . . . the person we love most on this earth."

While the Pope was hospitalized, del Portillo did his best to visit St. Peter's every day to pray for him. He would say the joyful mysteries of the Rosary in the car on the way, stop briefly in the square to say the Creed while looking toward the Holy Father's apartment, say the sorrowful mysteries on his way back, and the glorious mysteries after getting home.

After an initial recovery, John Paul II suffered a relapse and had to be hospitalized again in June. Del Portillo redoubled his prayer. On July 15 he was able to visit the Pope. Del Portillo told the ailing Pontiff, who had a high fever, that his sufferings were like a caress from the Blessed Virgin because they brought him closer to God; if illness is a treasure, he added, the illness of the Pope means even greater riches for him and the Church. The Pope replied simply, "That's exactly what I think."

Another indication of their closeness occurred one day when del Portillo was having dinner with the Pope. John Paul II asked, "Have you ever seen the devil?" When he answered, "No, Holy Father, but I touch him every day," the Pope said, "The same thing happens to me."

The friendship also had lighthearted moments. On one occasion Don Alvaro told John Paul that Escrivá had been accustomed to imagining himself wrapped in his cloak saying the Rosary with the pope. John Paul asked, "Does his successor do the same?" The answer: "His successor does the same, but without the cloak." Another time, when Mother Teresa was with them, John Paul asked her and Don Alvaro, "Why does the press always talk well about Mother Teresa, but not about Opus Dei or me?"

In July 1992 John Paul II was hospitalized again for what turned out to be a benign intestinal tumor. Del Portillo learned of the hospitalization as he arrived in Spain from a visit to Switzerland. Although in poor health and exhausted from his travel, he decided to return to Rome immediately: A son should stay close to his sick father, he explained. At the airport, a member of the Work noticed Don Alvaro's fatigue and urged him to take care of himself. He replied: "The truth is, my son, that I am indeed very tired. But we have done our duty."

Acting on the Pope's Wishes

Throughout his years as head of Opus Dei, del Portillo was anxious to respond in practical ways to the Pope's wishes, whether they involved the whole Church or specifically affected Opus Dei. He was eager to see Opus Dei have a presence in the Far East, and as soon as possible in China, but when he mentioned this to John Paul II, the Pope remarked that he was particularly concerned about Scandinavia. So del Portillo began at once to focus on that region. A few days later, in his Christmas greetings to members of the Work, he asked them to pray especially for Opus Dei's future apostolate there. Soon after he traveled to Norway, Finland, Sweden, and Denmark to explore possibilities and pray for the future apostolic activities of the Work. Del Portillo knew perfectly well how hard it would be for Opus Dei to put down roots in countries where there were very few Catholics, but the obstacles were far outweighed by the Pope's desires. Once the first centers were opened in the Nordic countries, he followed their progress particularly closely and lent his personal support, traveling there repeatedly, even in midwinter, to encourage the fledgling efforts.

These initiatives in northern Europe formed part of Opus Dei's larger response to John Paul II's call for a new evangelization of Europe and North America. When the Pope requested Opus Dei's collaboration, del Portillo immediately asked the members of its international governing bodies to pray for this intention. In December 1985 he wrote a long pastoral letter urging members and cooperators to take the Holy Father's desire very seriously and redouble their apostolic efforts. Repeatedly del Portillo traveled throughout Europe in order to stimulate Opus Dei's apostolate. He organized two weeklong meetings in Rome and two similar meetings in Spain to plan new efforts in Europe and America.

In 1994, shortly before his death, del Portillo learned that John Paul II would like Opus Dei to begin apostolic work in Kazakhstan, a geographically remote, largely Muslim country in central Asia, where Catholics are less than 2 percent of the population. It is unlikely that del Portillo or any of his collaborators had ever thought of beginning activities there, but upon learning of the Pope's interest, he commissioned studies of how to do that as soon as possible.

Del Portillo knew that in some circles his unwavering fidelity to the Pope would be criticized, but that did not matter to him. He once said, "Maybe people will say that this is worshiping the Pope. . . . We don't care what they say. We have the pride of knowing that we are children of God and children of the Pope as well, since he is the common father of all Christians."

CHAPTER 19

Finding a Safe Harbor

O ne of del Portillo's primary responsibilities upon becoming head of Opus Dei was to continue the founder's effort to obtain a satisfactory legal status for the Work. He feared, though, that an immediate request to change Opus Dei's legal status might be misinterpreted by people unaware of Escrivá's efforts as an inappropriate attempt by his successor to make major changes. In his first audience with Pope Paul VI, he said he thought it would be prudent to do nothing for a while. The Holy Father agreed; but in an audience in June 1978, he urged moving ahead. Del Portillo concurred that the time was ripe, but before a formal request could be submitted, Pope Paul VI died.

Early Steps

The death of the pope who had just encouraged moving forward was undoubtedly a setback, but the election of Cardinal Luciani—Pope John Paul I—was a hopeful development. Just a few days after his election, as we have seen, the new Pope unofficially communicated to del Portillo his desire to reach a prompt solution to the question of Opus Dei's legal status. He also urged the Congregation for Religious and Secular Institutes promptly to begin a study of the question. Del Portillo prayed and called on the members to pray.

The unexpected death of Pope John Paul I came as yet another blow for del Portillo, but he responded to this new setback by saying repeatedly a short prayer he had learned from Escrivá: *Omnia in bonum* ("Everything is for the good"), a condensed version of Saint Paul's admonition to the early Christians at Rome that "for those who love God, all things work together unto good" (Romans 8:28).

The election of Cardinal Wojtyla was a new source of encouragement. A few weeks later, the secretary of state communicated to del Portillo that the Holy Father considered "resolution of the question of the juridical status of Opus Dei a necessity that cannot be postponed." It seemed that the long-sought legal solution was imminent, but four more years of disappointments, prayer, sacrifice, and work and still lay ahead.

Setbacks

In preparation for the fiftieth anniversary of the foundation of the women's branch of Opus Dei, del Portillo proclaimed a new Marian year in the Work. When in Rome, he went daily to some church dedicated to Our Lady to pray the Rosary. When traveling outside Rome, he made a point of a visiting local shrines and churches dedicated to Mary— literally hundreds of them. Repeatedly, he directed requests for members of the Work to offer prayers and sacrifices for this intention.

In early January 1979 del Portillo asked the Congregation for Religious and Secular Institutes for permission to contact other organs of the Holy See, including the Congregation for Bishops, to request the legal transformation of Opus Dei. Having received that permission, he presented a formal request. In June, however, the cardinals who were members of the Congregation for Bishops decided that the change was not justified. Technically, their decision was took the form of a *dilata* (that is, to put the matter off to an unspecified later date). Del Portillo did not let himself become discouraged. On July 13, he wrote St. John Paul II, suggesting that the *dilata* should be interpreted not as a command to stop work on the project but as an invitation to Opus Dei to continue studying and preparing its statutes.

He continued working diligently for the new legal status. His successor, Bishop Echevarría, describes his efforts as involving "interviews, trips to various countries, clarification of the issues for the people who had to study the matter without interfering in their decisions, and, above all, much prayer and expiation, carried out with constant joy." The bishop adds that those with whom he had dealings "sensed not only the amiability and simplicity with which he acted, but also the fortitude of someone who is proposing a project in which the only goal is to give glory to God and serve the Church."

Soon he succeeded in convincing the congregation that further study was needed. But, even more, he converted the prefect of the congregation, Cardinal Baggio, and the Archbishop of Vienna, Cardinal König, into avid supporters. Cardinal König later wrote: "At first, I had thought that it was merely a caprice, and that there was no need to open up a new juridical path in the Church. Nonetheless, thanks to his explanations, I realized that Opus Dei was such a new phenomenon that it needed a new legal suit. I came to be an advocate of del Portillo's intention among my fellow cardinals."

New Difficulties

Vatican study had no sooner resumed than a new difficulty arose which the undersecretary of the congregation described as "diabolical." Someone stole a number of the documents from the congregation and sent bishops and newspapers around the world a partial and tendentious account composed of phrases taken out of context and reassembled to create a false picture. It made it seem that Opus Dei was trying to escape control by the diocesan bishops, and even to dictate to them, by becoming a "universal diocese," a sort of "little Church within the Church."

The Congregation for Bishops sent a note to the Vatican representatives in all countries where Opus Dei had an institutional presence, deploring what had happened and clarifying matters. Del Portillo reacted serenely but energetically, visiting Church leaders and giving instructions to Opus Dei directors around the world about how to explain the situation to bishops who might have been deceived. Above all, he prayed and asked others to pray. One of his close collaborators recalls his analysis like this: "Whenever something was done in this area, the devil grows angry and tries to stop it, but we were already prepared for that and had to keep going forward praying, praying." Following the example of Escrivá, he prayed even for those who were responsible for what had happened. "If someone mistreats us," he explained, "I count him among our benefactors."

Further Study

Despite this attempt to derail the process, in November, at del Portillo's suggestion, the Holy See established a joint commission of three Vatican representatives and three representatives of Opus Dei to study the issue further. Over the course of a year, the commission met twenty-five times and prepared a 600-page report that the prefect of the Congregation for Bishops submitted to John Paul II on April 4, 1981. The Pope promised to respond by May 16, but on May 13, the feast of Our Lady of Fatima, he was shot and almost killed in St. Peter's Square.

The Pope's recovery did not go well, and on June 20 he had to be hospitalized a second time. While still in the hospital, he informed the prefect of the bishop's congregation that he had reviewed the commission report before the attempt on his life and wanted a special high-level commission, eventually made up of eight cardinals, to study it.

Once again, an anonymous group stole documents from the congregation and used them to prepare a pamphlet in English, attributing it to "A Member of Opus Dei Who Works in the Vatican." The pamphlet, sent to bishops around the world, repeated the accusation that Opus Dei was trying to become a "parallel Church." Once again del Portillo set patiently to work, pointing out that the proposed statutes being studied by the special commission made it clear that making Opus Dei a personal prelature would not change its relations with bishops.

A director of the women's branch of Opus Dei who was in close contact with del Portillo at this time recalls that even in these painful circumstances, he never seemed "impatient or annoyed with the causes or persons who gave rise to the difficulties. On the contrary, they were for him a stimulus to abandon himself more completely in the hands of God, and to help the other faithful of the Work to see these events with a great deal of supernatural vision, praying, and pardoning."

Asked around this time how the process was going, Don Alvaro gave an answer reflecting his attitude from the start: "It's going very well, my son, because the Lord is the best of fathers, and a good father always hears his son's petitions. He has answered our prayers from the first moment. But what is worth a lot, costs a lot. If God sometimes wants to put off the concrete realization of what he has already granted us, he does it to test and strengthen our faith, our hope, and our love, to purify our humility, to strengthen our spirit. . . . It is going very well. We are praying a lot. If our

Lord puts off giving it to us, that is very good because we come closer to him and are very united. In the meantime, let this unanimous petition continue rising to heaven."

This storm also passed. On September 26, 1981, the commission of cardinals issued a favorable report. In early November, St. John Paul II told the prefect of the congregation he had decided to make Opus Dei a personal prelature after informing the bishops in dioceses where it was working. The information went to some 2,000 bishops in thirty-nine countries, and about 400 of them responded over the next six months. Only thirty-eight raised objections or asked for clarifications of some point. Although Vatican practice did not require it, John Paul II asked that the congregation reply to each of them over the prefect's signature.

Approval

Finally on August 5, 1982, the Holy Father told Cardinal Baggio he had decided to move ahead. The cardinal officially communicated the Pope's decision to del Portillo on August 19. The only steps remaining now seemed to be setting a date and preparing an official comment for publication in the Vatican newspaper, *L'Osservatore Romano*. Don Alvaro hoped the decision would be announced on August 21, the feast of St. Pius X, Opus Dei's intercessor for its relations with the Holy See, but day came and went without an announcement. So many important events in the life of Opus Dei had taken place on feasts of the Blessed Virgin that del Portillo confidently expected an announcement the next day, the feast of the Queenship of Mary. But that day also came and went with no announcement. People around del Portillo grew concerned, but he remained serene. Finally, on August 23, the Vatican made the official announcement.

Someone who worked with del Portillo remarked that
it seemed strange that the announcement had not come on
either of the two feast days but had instead been made on
"just any day." "No, my son," del Portillo replied, "it's not
just any day! It is the anniversary of the divine locution to
our Father! This is the great mercy of God which we were
waiting for." Eleven years earlier, on August 23, 1971,
Escrivá had heard in his soul "*Adeamus cum fiducia ad thro-
num gloriae ut miscericordiam consquamaur* [Let us go with
confidence to the throne of glory to obtain mercy]." These
were the words of Hebrews 4:16, except that the scriptural
text says "throne of grace" rather than of "glory." Escrivá
took the throne of glory to be the Blessed Virgin Mary. And
now she had answered so many years of confident prayer.

But again there was a delay. While announcing the Pope's
decision, the Holy See said official publication of the documents would be delayed "for technical reasons." Del Portillo
was not disturbed. On September 29 he wrote a Vatican official that this latest twist was "the grain of salt that gives fla-
vor; it is the Holy Cross."

The fall of 1982 brought a new campaign of calumnies
against Opus Dei, perhaps in an attempt to reverse the papal
decision. The aim was to link the Work to two scandals then
on the front pages of the Italian press, one involving P2, a
secret Masonic Lodge which had lost its charter years earlier but continued to operate and which was charged with
involvement in many crimes, and the other the murder of
Roberto Calvi, the president of a large bank who was found
dead after the bank failed. Although the allegations of Opus
Dei involvement had no basis in fact, they were widely
repeated in the press. "It is clear," del Portillo commented,
"that the devil wants to stir up the waters."

He called for even more prayer. "We are in the last centi-
meters of a 100-meter race," he told a group of his daughters.

On November 18 he began a novena of visits to shrines and churches dedicated to the Blessed Mother to ask that the final step be taken to transform Opus Dei into a personal prelature. And if at the end of the novena the final step still hadn't been taken, he said, "it will be a sign that we have to continue praying *fiat voluntas tua* [your will be done] (Mt 6:10). We will continue praying and saying, 'How good God is. He makes us pray even more.'" Finally, on November 26 Cardinal Baggio told del Portillo the Pope had created the personal prelature of Opus Dei and named him prelate. The official announcement was made the next day and published on November 28 in *L'Osservatore Romano*.

Final Steps

In a long letter to the members dated November 28, 1982, Del Portillo stressed that establishing Opus Dei as a prelature would bring many benefits, particularly the reinforcement of the Work's unity, the reaffirmation of its secularity, and a greater facility in apostolic activity. In fact, he said, the long and difficult process itself had also been a great good. "The Work, 'firm, compact, and secure,' closely united to our Father in the same intention, has prayed, has suffered, has hoped, and has worked. And this has been an immense good for Opus Dei and for the entire Church, because the only thing that moves us is a spirit of service to this good Mother." Like everything else that happened to Opus Dei, del Portillo wrote, these years of hope and suffering had been "permitted by God so that we may be good sons of his."

He went on to specify in more detail the benefits Opus Dei had derived from the painful process: "We have learned to work looking only to God, without hoping for any recompense on earth. We have learned to love those who for whatever reason did not understand, or did not want to understand, our way. We have learned to have patience and to pardon easily when some people—moved by the devil or ingenuously mistaken—carried out tenacious campaigns of calumny against us. Our Lord has confirmed us in a great love for all those who work for him, understanding and appreciating truly the generosity and the sacrifice of so many good souls—priests, religious, laypeople—who serve the Church. The Lord has urged us to love the Pope more each day. How many long hours our Father spent praying for the Roman Pontiff and what an 'injection of Romaness' he gave the entire Work! We have felt the urgency and the duty of praying more intensely for all the bishops, and we have given ourselves, with greater desire for unity, in service of the dioceses where we work."

Consistent with del Portillo's generous spirit, the prayers of the faithful at the solemn Mass of thanksgiving which he celebrated included a petition "for all our benefactors, and for all those who in one way or another have tried to impede or make difficult the journey of Opus Dei—for, in imitation of our Father, we not only forgive them with all our hearts, but we regard them, too, as benefactors." The response: "May the Lord, in the richness of his mercy, fill them with true goods in this life and grant them heavenly glory."

To express Opus Dei's gratitude to God and to the Blessed Virgin, he declared a Year of Thanksgiving. He also expressed gratitude to Pope John Paul: "Thank you, Holy Father, because in this way you have made our path towards sanctity and our service to the universal Church and to the local churches and their pastors more secure. We will try to pay this debt of gratitude with even more abundant prayer for you. Down through the ages all the souls that the Lord sends to his Opus Dei will do the same." He traveled to Vienna, Cologne, and Switzerland to thank Cardinals König and Höffner and Bishop Deskur for their roles in the process.

The last remaining step was publication of the formal papal document, known as a Bull. Now another potential difficulty arose when, with the publication of the new code of canon law in late January 1983, some canonists maintained that the lay faithful of prelatures were not really the prelatures' members. Had this interpretation prevailed, it would have undermined the entire structure of Opus Dei. Del Portillo therefore wrote to the deputy secretary of state, saying that the issuance of "a Bull with inaccurate expressions" would make it necessary for him "to have recourse to the Holy Father to rectify them" and would be harmful to the Pope's authority.

The final text of the Bull, handwritten on parchment, was finalized in early March, without any of the "inaccurate expressions" del Portillo had feared and was promulgated in a solemn ceremony on March 19, 1983, thus bringing to a close the decades-long process of finding an appropriate legal home for Opus Dei. Escrivá had begun the process and entrusted it to del Portillo. Thanks to his prayer, sacrifice, fortitude, and unwavering confidence in God and the Blessed Virgin, it was now complete.

Several years later, a medal was created to commemorate the event. Del Portillo at first rejected a design showing his own profile next to that of the founder. Fr. Javier eventually convinced him with the argument that it was a way of underlining continuity. "Although it makes me blush," del Portillo said, "I decided that since the less important figure is eclipsed by the more important one, it could stay."

Prelate Bishop

A personal prelature is not a diocese, but it does form part of the hierarchical structure of the Church, and the role of its prelate is similar in many ways to that of a diocesan bishop.

Shortly after Opus Dei's transformation into a personal prelature, the papal master of ceremonies told del Portillo that at Vatican liturgical events he should wear a ring and a pectoral cross as bishops do. Rumors began to circulate that he would be ordained a bishop very soon.

Hearing of the rumors, del Portillo requested an audience with the Holy Father. When the two men met, he pointed out that for years he had asked people to pray and make sacrifices so that God would give Opus Dei the legal status suited to it. "If now I am named a bishop, the devil can make some people think that I have asked for so many prayers in order to become a bishop. That is not true, but I do not want to scandalize anyone. I cannot therefore, Holy Father, accept." If the Holy See nevertheless considered it essential that the prelate be a bishop, he said he would resign. John Paul II understood and told him not to be concerned.

Although there were compelling reasons for the prelate of Opus Dei to be a bishop and del Portillo prayed that his successor might in fact be one, he continued to think he should not become a bishop himself. In late 1990, however, he was told the Holy Father wanted to ordain him and asked that he accept. His vicar general emphasized that this was not a question of personal recognition but something that would make the prelature more effective in the service of God. He also pointed out that for the first prelate to be a bishop would make it easier for his successors to be bishops. Don Alvaro wrote the Holy Father accepting the nomination.

When he told the members of the Work living in Villa Tevere about his upcoming ordination, he spoke as if it were something that would happen to someone else. "The prelate will receive the Sacrament of Orders in its fullness. There will be a new outpouring of the Holy Spirit on the head of the Work and, because of the communion of the saints, in some way on all of Opus Dei. It will move the Work forward all over the world. It will be a great gift of God, because in this way the prelate will form part of the college of bishops and will be a successor of the apostles."

Del Portillo, along with eleven others, was ordained bishop by St. John Paul II on January 6, 1991, in St. Peter's Basilica. As he lay prostrate on the floor during the litany of the saints, he thought, "We are poor worms, poor sinful men. But an outpouring of the Holy Spirit will descend upon us and give us the fortitude necessary to be successors of the apostles." Insistently he prayed, "That we be faithful, that we be faithful." Preaching at a solemn Mass the next day, he insisted on the same point: "The only thing worthwhile is to live a coherent life when we have responded yes to our Lord. Let us make up our minds to be faithful."

CHAPTER 20

BEATIFICATION OF THE FOUNDER

Having lived so many years close to Escrivá, del Portillo was convinced of the founder's sanctity, and the conviction only grew as he read the letters that flooded in after his death. Over and over again, people from all over the world declared themselves certain he had been a great saint.

First Steps

Under the rules in effect when Escriva died, a beatification cause could not be introduced until at least five years after the person's death, but there was much to be done in the intervening years. At del Portillo's direction, small cards were printed with a picture of the founder, a brief biographical sketch, and a prayer for private devotion. Translated into many languages, they were distributed throughout the world. Del Portillo insisted on the importance of recording favors thought to have been received through Escrivá's intercession, and soon a steady stream of testimonials began arriving in Rome. Many concerned small, more or less unremarkable occurrences, but a number told of truly striking happenings, and some were conceivably miraculous.

Del Portillo organized a team, headed by Fr. Flavio Capucci, an Italian priest of Opus Dei who would eventually be named postulator of the cause, to collect and index documentation for a future process of beatification, including the founder's published and unpublished writings and correspondence, notes others had taken of his preaching and things said in get-togethers and on other occasions, testimonies about his life, and written recollections of people who knew him. It was obvious from the beginning that this would be a huge task, but just how enormous became clear only with time.

The legislation governing beatification at the time required that a number of bishops and other church leaders ask the Holy See to open a cause. Many cardinals and bishops, as well as people from all walks of life who had known the founder or known about him and his writings, spontaneously wrote the Pope requesting his canonization. But del Portillo encouraged the members of Opus Dei to suggest doing so to others. For instance, he asked Fr. Joseph Muzquiz, one of the first three priests of Opus Dei, to visit bishops in Sierra Leone, Liberia, Ivory Coast, Ghana, and Upper Volta (today, Burkina Faso) to speak with them about the founder and suggest writing to the Holy See.[1]

Opening the Cause

In 1980 Opus Dei officially asked the Congregation for the Causes of the Saints to open Escrivá's cause of beatification and canonization. Although it was customary to celebrate such an event with a solemn Mass and press releases, del Portillo considered it more in keeping with Opus Dei's spirit of personal and collective humility not

---

1. Eventually, letters were received from sixty-nine cardinals, 241 archbishops, 987 bishops, and forty-one general superiors of religious orders, as well as from heads of state and of government, leading figures in the world of culture, the arts, science, and finance, and many ordinary people.

to do so. He preferred "to give thanks to God, because it is something very good for the Church and for the Work, and to remain silent."

The first stage of a process of beatification and canonization is collecting testimony, primarily from people who knew the individual. Because the founder had lived a good part of his life in Spain and almost three decades in Rome, two tribunals were formed to gather testimony, one in Rome and one in Madrid. Ninety-two witnesses, more than half of whom did not belong to Opus Dei, were called to testify. Between them, the two tribunals held almost a thousand sessions to hear witnesses. In view of the amount of information del Portillo had to offer, the Roman tribunal decided to take his testimony in writing rather than orally. It ran to more than 2,000 typewritten pages. The transcribed declarations of the other witnesses covered close to 11,000 pages. Documents from 390 public and private archives filled sixteen volumes. The founder's writings, together with transcripts of his preaching and other statements, occupied 13,000 pages.

The information collection phase ended in November 1986. The Holy See then designated a Dominican priest, together with the postulator, to prepare an extensive report on the life of the founder and how he lived the virtues. Because of the enormous quantity of material that had been collected, del Portillo formed a team of theologians, canonists, historians, and computer experts to assist in preparation of the official report or *positio*. He followed their work closely and set demanding deadlines for the various phases of the task. In June 1988 the 6,000-page *positio* was completed. Calling it a product of "extraordinarily rigorous critical methodology," Cardinal Palazzini, head of the Congregation for Causes of the Saints, said he knew of no other similar document "as complete, as extensive, and as analytic as this." He might have added that it was a reflection of del

Portillo's care and interest and the high standards he set for everyone involved in the project.

After studying the *positio*, the Congregation for the Causes of the Saints issued a decree declaring that the founder had lived the virtues to a heroic degree. Del Portillo was delighted, but in informing the Work's members, he said the declaration "should never serve as fuel for vanity. It should, rather, give us a greater sense of responsibility." In July 1991, in a decree approved by the Pope, the Holy See certified that a miracle had been worked through the founder's intercession.[2]

The Beatification

A few months later, the Holy Father announced that the ceremony of beatification would take place on May 17, 1992. As a way of preparing, del Portillo proclaimed a new Marian year to help his sons and daughters "live the beatification of our Father, hand-in-hand with holy Mary, with the desire for renewal . . . with a personal conversion." He repeated this theme frequently in the months that followed. In March, he wrote a 100-page pastoral letter, in the form of a commentary on the mysteries of the Rosary, setting out a detailed program of vocational fidelity. Less than a month before the ceremony, he wrote: "In this final sprint, I ask you to make an even greater effort in dealing with Our Lady, trying to spend the next two weeks hand-in-hand with Holy Mary and St. Joseph." It was a prescription he followed himself, saying in one get-together that "to have dealt so closely with a person who was on his way to the altars shakes me up."

---

2. The miracle involved the cure in 1976 of a seventy-year-old Carmelite nun who suffered from multiple illnesses including metastasized cancer, gastric ulcers, a hiatus hernia, and anemia. The tumor on her left shoulder had reached the size of an orange and her doctors had given up all hope of her recovering health. After her sisters prayed to St. Josemaría, she was completely cured.

Del Portillo paid close attention to the event's organization. To ensure vigorous singing by the congregation during the Mass in St. Peter's Square, he had the music recorded and sent to Opus Dei centers around the world. And knowing most people in attendance would be far from the altar in spots without seating or shade, he suggested bringing a folding chair, binoculars, and an umbrella to ward off the implacable Roman sun.

* * *

Although the months leading up to the beatification were a joyful time for del Portillo, it was mixed with suffering. A small but vocal group of ecclesiastics criticized the Pope's decision to beatify the founder and accused Opus Dei of manipulating the cause. *Newsweek* magazine and other media took note of the criticism.[3] Del Portillo reacted with his usual peace and calm, taking steps to clarify the facts while avoiding polemics or criticism of those behind the campaign. In a letter to the head of Opus Dei in Spain, where the attacks were particularly virulent, he wrote: "Be cheerful and serene. Live *in laetitia* [in joy] with the little cross that we now have to bear. . . . We are receiving one more proof, if more were needed, of our Father's sanctity." When the postulator of the cause told him of the death of a former religious who was one of those responsible for the campaign, del Portillo asked, "Have you prayed for his soul?"

Beatification day was splendid and sunny. An enormous crowd—members, cooperators, and friends of Opus Dei as well as admirers of Sister from Josephine Bakhita who would

---

3. Critics primarily focused on the rapidity with which the cause had proceeded. The process did proceed quickly, but this reflected changes made by John Paul II in the procedures precisely to speed up causes of beatification and canonization so as to present to the world more contemporary models of sanctity.

be canonized in the same ceremony[4]—packed St. Peter's Square and overflowed into the Via della Conciliazione leading to the Tiber River. Thirty-five cardinals and more than 200 archbishops and bishops were present, and some thirty countries sent official representatives.

At the time of the beatification, a priority project of the diocese of Rome was the building of new churches in outlying areas with large populations. Thanks to the generosity of many members and cooperators, Bishop del Portillo was able to present the Holy Father with plans for a new church to be dedicated to Blessed Josemaría Escrivá.

The day after the beatification, del Portillo celebrated a solemn Mass of Thanksgiving in St. Peter's Square. The site was the suggestion of Pope John Paul. Bishop del Portillo told a group of Opus Dei members, "I did not ask him. The idea had never even occurred to me, nor had any member of the Work thought about anything like it, because it has never been done. But it occurred to the Pope."

At the end of the Mass, the Holy Father rode around the square greeting the faithful gathered there. As the John Paul II approached the entrance to St. Peter's on foot, Bishop del Portillo sought to genuflect and kiss his hand, but the Holy Father prevented him and gave him a hug. At the end of the ceremony, John Paul quoted his own words about the need for "new models of sanctity and new testimonies of heroic virtues lived in the common ordinary conditions of human existence" (*Christifideles laici*, n. 17), and then pointed to Blessed Josemaría Escrivá as an example of

---

4. St. Josephine Bakhita was born in Sudan in 1869. She was kidnapped and sold as a slave and suffered repeated beatings and other mistreatment. Eventually she was purchased by the Italian Consul in Khartoum who took her with him when he returned to Italy. She was baptized in 1890 and entered the convent in 1893. She spent her entire life in a convent in a small town in the province of Venice working as a cook, seamstress, and doorkeeper. She soon became known for her gentle kindness. She died in 1947.

"Christian heroism in the exercise of common human activities." During the following two days, Masses of thanksgiving were concelebrated in churches throughout Rome in thirteen languages by a total of eighteen cardinals, sixty bishops, and hundreds of priests.

The beatification of the founder represented a solemn confirmation by the Church that the path opened up by Josemaría Escrivá is a sure path of sanctity. For del Portillo, who had been so close to Escrivá during the years when he was criticized and even called a heretic, it was an occasion of immense joy.

CHAPTER 21

FINAL DAYS

D el Portillo celebrated his eightieth birthday on March
11, 1994. In a letter to the faithful of Opus Dei, looking to his upcoming birthday, he called himself "a poor
beggar"and asked them "not to leave me without the charity of your daily prayer." In the homily he gave at Mass on
the day itself, he said, "I have received so many gifts that
they cannot be counted, so many caresses of Our Lady, my
Mother. . . . Thank you, Lord!" Recalling the founder's
motto, *nunc coepi* ("now I begin"), he declared: "Thanks
be to God and to the intercession of our Father, the fire of
love burns strongly in my heart. For that reason I feel very
young. . . . Being young in years is something simply phys-
iological that is not terribly important. What really matters
is the interior youthfulness that all the daughters and sons of
God in Opus Dei should always have. It is the youthfulness
of lovers—of those in love with God—who strive to make
their love grow more and more."

Pilgrimage to the Holy Land

Although he had long wanted to visit the Holy Land, he
had never done so because, following Escrivá's example,
he thought that the spirit of poverty implied traveling only
when there was an apostolic motive for the trip. Shortly

before his birthday, members of the General Council suggested it would be helpful for him to visit the newly opened Opus Dei center in Jerusalem. This cleared away the obstacles, and on his eightieth birthday he announced that he would soon make a pilgrimage to the Holy Land. Leaving the details to others, he specified only that he wanted to visit "the lake of Genesareth that our Lord crossed so often and row out onto the lake in a boat and make the prayer on the lake."

On March 14 he flew from Rome to Israel, accompanied by his two aides, Fr. Javier Echeverría and Fr. Joaquín Alonso. Though he had never been to the Holy Land, the places he was about to visit were all deeply familiar to him from sixty years of reading the New Testament daily and trying to put himself into the scenes of the gospel and participate in the events the evangelists narrated.

The pilgrimage was physically taxing and at times del Portillo showed signs of being tired and short of breath. But he also showed profound joy at being in the land blessed by Christ's presence. Visiting the scenes of our Lord's life, he remarked in Nazareth, "It seems easier to talk with God and consider the Lord's love for us [here]."

The pilgrimage began on March 15 in the Basilica of the Annunciation in Nazareth and ended on March 22 with Mass in the Church of the Cenacle, where Christ instituted the Eucharist. On March 16th they visited the Sea of Galilee, but car problems made them late arriving and kept them from making their afternoon meditation out on the lake, as del Portillo had hoped. He accepted the small disappointment with his usual good humor. Asked whether he wanted to try again next day, he said simply, "No, my son, it was just a whim." They made their meditation on the shore of the lake, near the rock said to be the one on which Our Lord laid the bread and fish he multiplied.

On March 17 they visited Cana, where Jesus turned water into wine, and Mount Tabor, where he was transfigured in the presence of Peter, James, and John. In the afternoon they returned to Jerusalem and prayed at Calvary and the Church of the Holy Sepulchre. The Holy Sepulchre, Bishop Echevarría recalled, "is so small that only six people can enter. We got in line, and the Father began to pray. From that moment on, he secluded himself in order to contemplate how much God has done for each one of us. When we got inside the Holy Sepulchre . . . we saw the rock where the body of Christ was laid. . . . The Father fell on his knees and was there for a long time with his hands, his arms, and his head resting on the stone. It was hard to leave that place because you could see that the Father was absorbed in prayer. . . . We were there quite a while until, thinking about the people who were waiting in line outside, we told the Father that it was time to go." The next day del Portillo returned to the Church of the Holy Sepulchre to celebrate Mass. He dedicated the entire day to meditating on the Passion in the Holy Sepulchre, the Church of the Agony, and the Garden of Olives.

On March 19, the feast of St. Joseph, they visited Christ's birthplace in Bethlehem, where del Portillo celebrated Mass in the Church of the Nativity. Later that day, he had a get-together with a group of members, cooperators, and friends of Opus Dei. There he exclaimed: "It is incredible. To be in the Holy Land . . . where Jesus was born and died, where he passed most of his earthly existence living a hidden life, without noise, working as a poor carpenter."

One of those attending the get-together was a police officer from another country, in Israel for anti-terrorism training. He thought poorly of the Church and priests, but he had accepted an invitation to attend primarily out of curiosity. Don Alvaro's comments and the simplicity with which he

spoke moved him deeply. The man underwent a profound
conversion that completely changed his life.

March 20th saw del Portillo in Bethany, the home of
Martha, Mary, and Lazarus, as well as in Ein Karem, thought
to be the place where Mary's cousin St. Elizabeth lived when
the Blessed Virgin visited her. He also took time to visit several
potential sites of centers in Jerusalem, as well as a possible
site for a conference center outside the city. In the afternoon,
he made his meditation in the Church of the Flagellation.

As he habitually did when traveling, he found time to
write postcards to friends, including the Castelli family.
From Nazareth, he sent postcards to his vicars throughout
the world, with a picture of the Grotto of the Annunciation
and a message saying, "*Ave Maria, gratia plena, Dominus
tecum* [Hail Mary, full of grace, the Lord is with you]. In this
holy place we are praying for you in an altogether special
way. Your Father embraces you and blesses you."

In the afternoon of his last full day in the Holy Land, del
Portillo met with a group of students from several Opus Dei
centers in the United States who were making a pilgrimage
to the Holy Land before attending the UNIV student congress scheduled to be held in Rome in a few days. He asked
them to pray a great deal for the Pope and a little bit for
him, and he encouraged them to be generous and fulfill the
will of God, whatever that might be for each of them. A high
school student said after the get-together, "I felt like I was
with a saint."

The trip ended March 22 with Mass in the Church of the
Cenacle. It would be his last Mass. He offered it as he did
every day, for the Pope and his intentions. Fr. Echevarría later
recalled, "I was impressed seeing the devotion with which he
put on the vestments. You could see that he was particularly
recollected and deeply moved. . . . He celebrated with great
piety. You could see that he was tired, because of his physical

fatigue, although perhaps also because of the emotion of being in that holy place. I can assure you that he lived these moments with great intensity, with a real madness of love."

At the airport, despite his obvious fatigue, he was, as usual, serene, patient, and good-humored during the typically lengthy Israeli exit interview. On board the private jet that an Italian cooperator had provided for the trip, he chatted with the crew members. When he learned that the copilot was engaged, he asked to see a picture of his fiancée. Several families met him at the airport and gave him a bouquet that he at once said he would give to the Blessed Virgin. When he reached Villa Tevere, he briefly greeted the members of the General Council and the Central Advisory Board, had a light supper, examined his conscience, and went to bed.

Death

At 3:10 a.m. on the morning of March 23, he felt a sudden sharp pain. Calling Father Echevarría, he told him serenely, "My heart is out of control." The doctor arrived quickly and, realizing that the situation was very serious, told him so. Even so, he retained his calm and good humor, teasing the doctor about the bathrobe he was wearing. Father Echevarría gave him sacramental absolution and the anointing of the sick. The doctor did all that he could, but in vain. At four o'clock in the morning, he pronounced Don Alvaro dead.

At 6:30 a.m., Msgr. Echevarría called the Pope's secretary and asked him to inform His Holiness of del Portillo's death. John Paul II said that he would offer the Mass he was about to celebrate for the repose of Don Alvaro's soul. The same day, he sent condolences in which he spoke of del Portillo's "life full of priestly and episcopal zeal, the example of fortitude and confidence in divine Providence that he constantly offered, his fidelity to the See of Peter, and his generous

ecclesial service as the closest collaborator and worthy successor of Blessed Josemaría Escrivá."

Del Portillo once wrote of death: "When we make the
great leap, God will be waiting for us, to give us a big hug
and let us look upon his face forever and ever and ever. And
since our God is infinitely wonderful, we will be discovering
new marvels for all eternity. We will be filled without being
satiated. We will never get tired of tasting his infinite sweetness." That presumably is how it was and is for him.

In a postcard from the Holy Land, del Portillo had asked
Pope John Paul's secretary to "present to the Holy Father
our desire of being *fideles usque ad mortem* [faithful unto
death] in the service of the Holy Church and of the Holy
Father." Don Alvaro was truly faithful unto death.

EPILOGUE

On January 2004, at the request of the prelate of Opus Dei, Bishop Echevarría, and the vicar of Rome, Cardinal Ruini, the Congregation for the Causes of the Saints gave permission to open del Portillo's cause of beatification and canonization. The Diocese of Rome and the Opus Dei prelature formed tribunals to receive testimony about his life. The two tribunals collected testimony from 168 witnesses, including thirty cardinals, eighteen archbishops and bishops, four priests, and one monk.

* * *

On February 2010 the Franciscan priest in charge of its preparation presented an official 2,500-page report (the *positio*) based on the witnesses' testimony and extensive archival research. After studying the report, first the theological consultants of the Congregation for the Causes of the Saints and then the cardinals and bishops who are its members concluded in 2012 that Don Alvaro had practiced the virtues heroically. Based on their report, Pope Benedict XVI authorized the congregation to promulgate a decree on the heroic virtues of Bishop Alvaro del Portillo.

Meanwhile, the congregation was also studying a miraculous cure attributed to his intercession. Days after his birth, in August 2003, a Chilean boy named José Ignacio underwent surgery for an intestinal hernia. In the course of the operation, the surgeons discovered that he also had a serious heart defect. He was operated on for that two days later. The operation went well, but several days later the boy went into cardiac arrest and suffered a major hemorrhage. The family prayed intensely to Don Alvaro. The doctors worked to revive him, but without success. After more than half an hour, they began to stop their efforts and told his mother he was dead. Suddenly José Ignacio's heart began to beat more strongly and quickly, and soon it was functioning normally. Considering the circumstances, the doctors expected him to have very serious brain damage, but he suffered no adverse consequences and is today a healthy boy living a normal life.

On July 5, 2013, Pope Francis signed a decree recognizing Javier's recovery as a miracle worked through the intercession of Don Alvaro. This cleared the way for his beatification, which is scheduled to take place in Madrid on September 27, 2014.

INDEX

Santander, Spain, 27
Saragossa, Spain, 27, 58, 92
Satan, 126
Scandinavia, 198
School of Civil Engineering, 18
School of Public Works Engineering Technology, 17
Scripture, 77
second general congress (1956), 107–8
Second Vatican Council, 109, 114–22, 124–25, 126, 132, 144, 176, 186–87
Second World War, 51, 58, 72, 80, 94
secular institutes, 88, 128, 129–30, 134
Seville, Spain, 27
sexuality, 127
sick, concern for the, 156–58
Singapore, 163, 182
Society of Jesus, 65
   See also Jesuits
Solano, Jesús, 177
The Soul of the Apostolate (Chautard), 33
Spain
   anticlericalism in, 24, 29, 37
   anti-religious legislation in, 22–23
   Catholicism, Catholics in, 21
   Communism in, 25
   education in, 10–11
   Falange in, 24–25, 64, 65
   Franco government in, 64
   Nationalist uprising in, 26–27, 27–28
   political and social background in, 21–29
   Republican government in, 25, 27, 41

Spanish Civil War and, 18, 20, 25, 27–29, 41–49, 58, 63
Spanish Civil War in, 50–56
Spanish Civil War, 18, 20, 25, 27–29, 36–40, 41–49, 50–56, 58, 63
The Spanish Civil War (Payne), 21n1
Special Tribunal for the Suppression of Masonry and Communism, 64–65
spiritual childhood, 151
spiritual communion, 38
spiritual formation, 5, 7, 50, 78, 124, 160–62
spiritual life, xii, 50, 51, 60, 77, 80–81, 89
spiritual reading, 42, 153
Stations of the Cross, 12
Stein, Edith, 176
St. Vincent de Paul Society, 1, 15, 18
suffering, 42, 99, 123, 125–28, 168
Sweden, 163, 198

T

Taiwan, 163, 182
Tardini, Domenico, 86, 94, 97, 114
Tedeschini, Cardinal, 92, 93, 117
Teilhard de Chardin, Pierre, 127–28
Teresa Benedicta of the Cross, St., 176
Teresa of Avila, St., 33, 63, 77
Time magazine, 133
Tito, 104
Trinidad-Tobago, 163
Trinity, 153